D1116344

**Third Generation** · The Changing Meaning of Architecture

Philip Drew

# Third Generation

# The Changing Meaning of Architecture

# Praeger Publishers

New York · Washington · London

## Acknowledgement

Without the enthusiasm and support of Gerd Hatje, the idea of charting the profile of the Third Generation of modern architects would surely have foundered. The concept and formation of the work benefited greatly from his considerable experience as a publisher, involvement in and acute appreciation of the currents which enliven contemporary architecture. I would like to thank the house staff and in particular Axel Menges for his friendly sympathetic assistance, Mrs. Ursel Prehn who diligently collected the illustrations, and Mrs. Gisela Schlientz who courageously undertook to translate the text into German.

The author is deeply appreciative of the individual architects who gathered together and supplied the illustrations and whose critical interest was an important stimulus, especially Peter Cook, Ron Herron, Dennis Crompton and Frei Otto who were generous enough to explain their arguments. I am indebted to my wife Julie for her sympathetic criticism and tolerance of my infidelity in taking on the Third Generation as my second mistress. This book is dedicated to the new generation of architects who sought to raze the new prohibitions and bring architecture back into the arena of life.

Philip Drew

BOOKS THAT MATTER

# Contents

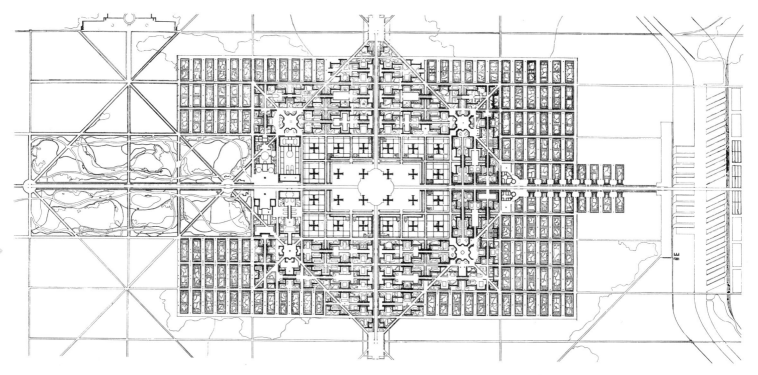

## Introduction

With the emergence of the third generation of architects, born between the two wars, the modern architecture movement entered a new phase of criticism, renewal and maturity. The exhibitionism of the second generation in the fifties, overshadowed by an ageing first generation, was symptomatic of their desperate search for an independent identity. Even the extreme longevity and creative force of the surviving first generation leadership was incapable of resisting the mounting pressures which required the overhaul of the ideological and stylistic foundations of the movement. The environmental recipes perfected by the first generation had been tried and their credibility exposed. The first generation's faith in rationalism and its authoritarian dictatorship of preconceived extrinsic patterns of order was incompatible with a living, changing environment.

The third generation does not present a monolithic, self-consistent architectural programme. Rather, it exhibits a new-found tolerance and mature insight into the complex contradictions of life. The new consciousness found in the architecture of the third generation confirms a significant change in the meaning of modern architecture, not merely as a set of opinions, information or values, but as a total configuration or construct. Architectural meaning in the present state is one in which differences are regarded as aspects of pluralism to be expressed in the creative process without inhibition. These architects represent a parliament of interests, with commitments so diverse and difficult as to defy any attempt to apply simplistic categories or announce revolutionary manifestoes. In order to function effectively, a parliament must submit to a consensus which utilizes free debate as an essential means of defining a democratic code for life. An uninhibited search for a democratic, intrinsic ordering of the environment imparts an unsuspected unity and flexibility of character to the third generation of modern architects.

The co-existence of the dual alliance of rational-geometric and organic-mystical patterns of environmental order (figs. 1, 2) characteristic of the first generation was replaced by a new hybrid which allied the organic conception of spontaneous intrinsic systems of order with geometry and mathematics. The subjective assumptions of rationalism were disclosed by the investigations of twentieth-century philosophy. Where it has survived in the third generation, the rationalistic point of view is joined to a rejuvenated classicism and mysticism which confirms the unwarranted assumptions of objectivity which so seduced the first generation mind.

The latent nihilism of Archigram's discussions points to a radical conception of order almost indistinguishable from disorder. They envisage a personalized anarchy lacking any superstructure of environmental order—or simply a spontaneous self-regulating chaos. The Japanese Metabolists share a similar tolerance towards disorder, which could explain the *rapport* existing between the two movements. The Japanese sense of order is wholly different from the Western concept, and is centred on the creation of potent symbols and the structuring of relationships between them powerful enough to contain the unrestrained chaos of random activity. The intense preoccupation of Japanese architects with the symbolic connotations of architectural form is proportional to the level of disorder within the Japanese urban setting.

The third generation turned to unselfconscious architecture as a primitive model and inspiration for intrinsic, organic systems of order. This is the line of development followed by Jørn Utzon, Moshe Safdie and Christopher Alexander.

The departure of Frank Lloyd Wright, Le Corbusier, Walter Gropius and Mies van der Rohe deprived a rising generation of modern architects of effective leadership. It is possible that they were the products of an heroic age, and that the present generation will manage without their heroes.

1, 2. Separate organic-mystical and rational-geometric responses were expressed by Frank Lloyd Wright's project for the Synagogue Beth Shalom in Elkins Park, Pennsylvania, 1956 (1), and Le Corbusier's Voisin plan for the centre of Paris, 1922 (2).

Around 1960, the ideas and interests which came to dominate the decade of the sixties made themselves felt. The new generation, the third to succeed in the chronology of the modern architecture movement, recall the twenties by their profound determination to reshape architecture according to the image and realities of their age.

This study is intended as an introduction to the ideas and architecture of a selected group of architects representing the third generation. Rather than attempt to describe the entire spectrum of third generation concerns and activities, with the inevitable superficiality which such a strategy implies, the discussion has been purposely focused on selected architects who best represent an important interest. By describing in some detail the ideas and projects of these individuals, it was thought that a more accurate and meaningful definition of third generation architecture could be drawn. This is only a start. A comprehensive bibliography of essential third generation sources has been included in an appendix, to assist interested readers to form their interpretation of the meaning and value of the new architecture.

The dangers of a revived mannerist aesthetic, growing out of the rediscovery of popular mass culture, threatens to sever architecture from reality. At the moment when the future of urban civilization is uncertain, the diversion of creative energy from the solution of real problems to the elaboration of an artificial aesthetic—no matter how sophisticated or clever it must appear under the present circumstances—is inappropriate. The fulfilment of architecture's human responsibilities is crucial to its continuing relevance.

Philip Drew, London, December 17, 1971

# Chapter 1 · The Uncertain Future

*'We find in the records of the antiquities of man that the human race has progressed with a gradual growth of population . . . what most frequently meets our view is our teeming population; our numbers are burdensome to the world, which can hardly supply us from its natural elements; our wants grow more and more keen, and our complaints more bitter in all mouths, while nature fails in affording us her usual sustenance. In very deed, pestilence, and famine, and wars, and earthquakes have to be regarded as a remedy for nations, as a means of pruning the luxuriance of the human race.'*[1]

Tertullian, a Carthaginian writing in the third century A.D.

Mankind's future is uncertain. The prospect of ecological catastrophe threatens to terminate the progress of civilization. It now seems that industrialization may be a more fundamentally disturbing force in world ecology than is population. Industrialization freed mankind from the constraints of pre-industrial agriculture, and modern medicine affected a sizeable reduction in the death rate. The appalling scale and complexity of the immediate ecological crises requires a comprehensive reappraisal of the role of industry. It is certain that resource depletion, pollution, crowding, famine, disease or some other equally destructive force will limit population and industrialization if they are not defused by effective counter measures. Exponential growth cannot long continue. If tragedy is to be avoided, man must move away from an exploitative growth orientated outlook.

Modern architecture developed from the deliberate efforts of the first European generation of modern architects to marry architecture and modern technology. The theoretical superstructure and aesthetic of the new movement reflected the intense determination of these early pioneers to incorporate selected features of science and technology in the new architecture. The first generation scavenged science and technology for levers to extricate architecture from the iron grasp of the past and launch it into the new machine age. Their task was to drag architecture into the twentieth century. The challenge facing the third generation is to see it safely through, and they now need to review those features of architectural ideology which were taken over from science and technology in the twenties.

Our present troubles go much deeper than the implementation of more effective programmes to control pollution or population growth. Western materialism has brought the world to the brink of disaster (fig. 1). It is necessary to rethink those values, and to restate architecture accordingly.

The decade of the twenties, which presided over the emergence of the new architecture, were turbulent times of political, economic and social upheaval. The problems of the day were highly visible. Today's problems are less apparent—though they penetrate the substrata of western consciousness and demand the substitution of community with nature for anthropocentrism. Fundamental to the new outlook is the recognition of the earth's finiteness, that many of the resources man depends upon are non-renewable, and that the delicate web of life may be irreparably damaged by his thoughtless extravagance. Architecture, as much as anything else, is subject to these ecological directives. In order to assess the nature of the transition involved, and the impact of this on the theory and practice of architecture, it is necessary to study in some detail the character and thrust of the prime forces which shape man's destiny.

Technology is the principal means whereby man has multiplied the earth's carrying capacity, at least temporarily. Europe's population increased by 350 percent during the two centuries accompanying industrialization (1750–1950). A fairly consistent correlation is evident between the intensity of industrialization, the rate of resource

1. Technological man's rapacious exploitation of the earth threatens to injure the delicate web of ecological relationships which sustain life.

depletion and levels of pollution. Convention holds that technology is neutral. Accordingly, the source of the trouble is the mis-management of the entire technological-human-political-economic-natural-complex. Such an explanation ignores the dynamic character of the interaction between technology and the cultural and ecological systems. For technology is deeply embedded in the cultural system, and demands placed upon it require appropriate and corresponding adjustments. The relationship of technology to man's cultural systems and the environment is not passive, rather, it is dynamic and engaged. Any account of the effect of technology on society and vice versa must take cognizance of this fact. Technology is hardly the compliant moll she is commonly supposed.

Technology is a state of Western mentality. Its creation tarried on a change of mind and its growth was sustained by the parallel appearance of appropriate dispositions and attitudes. The conception of nature was fundamental to the new mentality. Traditional Oriental civilizations acknowledged the interrelatedness of man and nature through the media of culture and social institutions. The patterns of life were founded on a sensitive symbiosis between man and nature. The subtle accommodation of man's needs with nature ensured the survival of both. The rational ideology which arose during the post-Renaissance period objectified nature, and this new frame of mind further estranged man.

The mental attributes of the new outlook necessitated a separation of nature from self. This separation treated nature as a foreign thing outside of, and hostile to the individual. The Renaissance exemplifies the three stages in the separation of nature from the self; beginning with the discovery of nature as an object of aesthetic contemplation, then as an object of exploration, and finally, as an object of exploitation. The machine arose out of the denial of the organic and living. Modern technology is rooted in the concepts of this rational ideology. It was to this same source that the founders of the modern movement turned in their attempt to modernize architecture.

The generation of the twenties confused their needs with the goals of the industrial system. They fondly imagined that the technologists shared their vision of an industrialized architecture. In 1923 Le Corbusier demanded that 'industry on the grand scale must occupy itself with building and establish the elements of the house on a mass production basis'[2], but industry remained unmoved by the prospect of renovating architecture. It chose instead to ignore the unsolicited attentions of architects. The failure of understanding was mutual. Gropius put forward the notion of houses fabricated from standardized mass-produced components (1909) and Corbusier enshrined it in the central litany of architectural ideology.

Corbusier's statements on the industrialization of architecture took the form of emotional harangues more appropriate to the trenches at Verdun than post-war reconstruction.

'We must create the mass-production spirit.
The spirit of constructing mass-production houses.
The spirit of living in mass-production houses.
The spirit of conceiving mass-production houses.'[3]

One wonders whether mass impregnation followed.

The sober realism of Moshe Safdie's estimate, taken from the vantage of four decades, contrasts with Corbusier's romantic faith in the industrial system (figs. 2, 3). 'It is dangerous to underestimate the difficulties of introducing mass production, closed-system techniques into housing. A house is much more complex than an aircraft. An aircraft can be clearly defined in terms of physical performance . . . a house is a physical problem, plus a complex social problem, plus a complex psychological problem. A house has to be publicly accepted . . .'[4]

2. Le Corbusier's romantic faith in the industrial system emerges from his picture of the New City where 'in the heart of the business city . . . the skyscrapers raise their heads, the town still remains green. The trees are kings; men, under their cover, live in the domain of proportion; the link nature-man is re-established'.

3. The ideal of mass production which the first generation aspired to took form with the prefabricated bathroom which Moshe Safdie engineered for Habitat '67.

Today, technology means many things. Christopher Alexander's decomposition of design problems, described in Chapter 2, is a model of the technological method. The shape of modern industry derives from technologies' habit of dividing and subdividing (decomposition of a problem into sets and sub-sets) (fig. 4) tasks into manageable units for the purposes of design and production. The finished elements must be combined (synthesis) into the finished product. The increasing complexity and sophistication of modern technology means that more time is taken to complete a task, and this necessitates a heavier commitment of capital. The allocation of time and money becomes more inflexible. Concomitant with the specialization of manpower and resources which follows from the increasing complexity of technology is organization. In sum, the increasing demand on time and capital, the loss of flexibility of this commitment through the needs of large-scale organization, and the problems of market performance under conditions of advanced technology increases the burden of planning. The goals of the industrial system, which are an expression of these technological imperatives, must be accommodated within the industrial society. These goals are various, and range from efficient production of goods and a steady expansion of output, to a steady expansion of consumption. The industrial system influences the social system by its unqualified commitment to technological change, its strong preference for goods rather than leisure, its desire to preserve the autonomy of the technostructure, and its need for a supply of trained and educated manpower.

The shape of modern industrial society is by no means arbitrary. To a large extent, it reflects the pressures within the industrial system which arise in part from the neces-

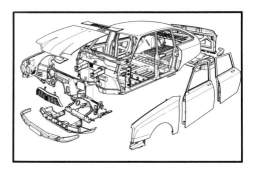

4. The habit of decomposing design and manufacturing briefs into manageable tasks is characteristic of industry at all levels. Citroen GS body and chassis sub-assemblies.

5. Patterns of light—not heavy masonry—define the environmental form and quality of Fremont Street in Las Vegas.

sities of advanced technology. Of fundamental importance for the future is the extent to which the modern industrial system can be adjusted to serve man's needs. Is modern man the victim of technological determinism? To what extent are economic growth, resource depletion and waste, planned obsolescence, social irresponsibility, pollution and armament races integral features of the industrial system? Is it possible to have one without the others? In *The New Industrial State*, John Galbraith asserts that:

'It is part of the vanity of modern man that he can decide the character of his economic system. His area of decision is, in fact, exceedingly small. He could conceivably decide whether or not he wishes to have a high level of industrialization. Thereafter, the imperatives of organization, technology and planning operate similarly . . . *Given the decision to have modern industry, much of what happens is inevitable and the same*'.[5] (author's italics)

The impact of the new technologies, especially electronic media, led to the rediscovery of architecture as experience (fig. 5). This new definition ignores the exclusive equation of architecture with monumental building, and attaches to it the sensible experience of form, space, and wholeness, regardless of semantic source. Few buildings transmit a message which is identifiably architecture. Likewise, other categories of environmental experience may occasion a nervous response which is unmistakably architectural. Thingvellir in Iceland (fig. 6) is a magnificent example of naturally-occurring architecture. Its architectural qualities were much appreciated by the Viking settlers who established their Althing (or national parliament) there in 980 A.D. Similarly electronic media, pneumatic and tent structures may occasion sensations which are recognizable as architecture. The exclusive identification of architecture with monumental building (figs. 8,9) has served to isolate it from life. The third generation, and more especially Archigram, have sought to restore architecture to life, to view it as a special type of environmental experience rather than as a special type of object.

The disadvantage of the old monumental type of architecture is its inability to respond to human needs and to change. The supreme flexibility, responsiveness and portability of the new electronic media was the occasion of some envy among the third generation. The impulse to restore architecture to the domain of human experience was labelled anti-architecture in recognition of its antipathy to the monumental. This is unfortunate, because it preserves the notion of architecture as a narrow category of objects. Architecture is experience, it is a part of life (fig. 7). American consumer technology, the wilder blandishments of automobile styling, plug-in, clip-on, throw-away, do-it-yourself and the accompanying advertising imagery have exercised a peculiar fascination on the English architectural *avant-garde*, dating back to the Institute of Contemporary Arts in the mid fifties. Archigram inherited this disposition and strengthened the connection. Throughout the sixties, they systematically built up a pattern vocabulary for the environment based on the imagery and processes of consumer mass-production (fig. 10). Warren Chalk explained Archigram's involvement in the following way:

'We are in pursuit of an idea, a new vernacular, something to stand alongside the space capsules, computers and throw-away packages of an atomic-electronic age.'[6] It will be remembered that Le Corbusier said much the same thing in the twenties. The flirtation with technology instituted by him and by C.I.A.M. (Congrès Internationaux d'Architecture Moderne) preoccupies Archigram. It is ironic that at this moment in history, when Americans are beginning to regard the techniques of planned obsolescence and managed consumption with increasing alarm, Archigram should seize upon them as the *modus operandi* of their thinking.

The work of James Stirling, John Andrews, Kiyonori Kikutake, and Kevin Roche

6. The presence of a unique landscape setting at Thingvellir in Iceland provided the essential architecture for early Viking parliaments.
7. An architecture for running, jumping and standing still; the quest for freedom in the sixties was equated with the flexibility and responsiveness of pneumatic environments.

8, 9. Almost indistinguishable from a genuine World-War II artillery bunker (bottom), Claude Parent's fortress of the faith, St. Bernadette in Nevers, France, 1963–4 (right), recalled the monumentality of traditional masonry architecture.

illustrates the prevalent third generation response, that of technological pragmatism. In essence, this involves accepting the present condition of technology and the relative primitiveness of building construction, and making something of it. Theirs is a craftsmanlike approach which sizes up the existing situation, appraises the opportunities and attempts to mould the architectural product in accordance with an individual creative vision. In Roche's case, this means expressing the extraordinary force of orthodox American industrialism. The principle of designing machine components with predetermined service lives for ease of maintenance (fig. 11)—a feature of aero-space engineering in which reliability is a crucial consideration—was incorporated in metabolist theory. In practice, this involves isolating short-life mechanical and service elements from the relatively durable structure and finishes to facilitate renewal of the architectural organism.

It is tempting to cast Frei Otto as a gifted technician, an expert designer of suspension structures, that hero of architectural mythology, the pure functionalist. Such an assessment detracts from Frei Otto's real achievement as an architect of rare sensitivity and technical accomplishment. Significantly, Frei Otto develops his designs through the use of a variety of modelling techniques, a medium which allows him to assess the structural and visual qualities of a project simultaneously. His commitment to experimental architecture and the progress he has already made is important in a world which desperately needs to use its diminishing resources to greater effect. In Utzon and Safdie, there is a coming together of minds bringing with it a common morphology of form and an identity of goals spanning twenty years—the difference in their ages. Utzon and Safdie begin with nature. For them it is the ultimate measure of architecture (fig. 12). Both come to technology with the determination to be its master, to tame its inhuman excesses and so attain the victory of infinite variety within repetitive systems. They are the true heirs to the idea which has haunted modern architects for half a century—to put architecture in the factory and so make it available to the masses.

Unselfconscious architecture—the example of the pueblos, Taxco and Mediterranean villages—contains the promise that an industrial architecture similarly conceived and dedicated to serving human needs could tap the immense productivity of the industrial system and avoid soulless monotony. At Puerto Rico, Safdie may realize that dream.

10. Archigram's contemporary pattern jargon incorporated the tower forms of petro-chemical installations.

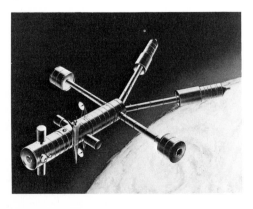

11. The flexibility of plug-in space capsules illustrates an essential feature of Metabolist theory.

Both Utzon and Safdie make demands on technology; they extend it beyond the limits of the known, challenging established ideas. At Sydney, Utzon asked that technology solve new problems, and Habitat was a similar experiment. Without the understanding of society that a new means must be found to pioneer the environment, and its willingness to dedicate funds for this purpose, architecture will continue to stagger aimlessly, doing things crudely.

Mankind is currently engaged in establishing the limits of the earth. The world is already running out of easily-mined ores and fuel for power for mass-production machinery and agricultural yields. Advanced societies have come to expect technology to solve their problems, and this works well when there are unlimited natural resources and geographical spaces for expansion; however, these conditions no longer prevail. It seems likely that societies with a high level of industrialization may be non-sustainable. They may be self-extinguishing if they exhaust the natural resources on which they depend. As agriculture reaches a space limit, as industrialization reaches a natural resource limit, and as both reach a pollution limit, population tends to catch up. The present underdeveloped countries may be in a better condition for surviving the forthcoming world-wide environmental and economic pressures than are the advanced countries. Even if technology is successful in reducing industry's dependence on natural resources, this will only serve to activate other environmental pressures such as pollution or population. The Dr. Strangeloves of science abound with prophecies of instant food and energy. Paul Ehrlich exposed the horrific irresponsibility of such fantasies with the observation:

'When you (the "prophets of agricultural Utopia") can adequately feed the 3.6 billion people we have now (1970)—including the 10,000,000 to 20,000,000 who are dying of starvation each year—come back and tell us how you'll feed the seven billion we'll have in the year 2,000.'[7]

The earth is running out of some very critical natural resources. And the demand shows no sign of abating; rather, it is increasing at an accelerating rate, and in many instances, no substitutes are foreseeable. Unless something drastic is done to reverse the present pattern of resource use, it will probably take one generation for resource depletion to become widespread and involve major raw materials such as oil and the common metals. At present rates of consumption, the known deposits of crude oil, natural gas, uranium, Tungsten, lead, zinc, tin, gold, silver and platinum will be exhausted by the end of the century. Aluminium, cobalt, nickel and manganese will probably last another century, and iron another two centuries. Reserves of coal and lignite will last 300 and 400 more years. The United States, which numbers six percent of the world's population, monopolizes thirty to thirty-five percent of its resources, and this could increase to fifty percent by 1980.

There are a number of alternatives to economic abstinence—producing and consuming less—which would alleviate the drain on natural resources. The principal strategies are recycling materials, increasing the lifespan of durable goods and substitution of renewable for non-renewable resources. The price of a raw material is determined primarily by the rate at which it comes on to the market. Commercial calculations ignore the social costs of disposal, pollution and replacement. Recycling in itself is insufficient to maintain economic processes. The pressures of fashion, planned obsolescence and routine style-changes, necessary under the existing economic system to maintain aggregate demand and sustain employment, mitigate against increasing the durability of commodities. The problem of resource depletion is not a technical problem—although it may require a reorientation of design priorities—it is a problem of reshaping political and economic institutions.

The quantity of resources used in building may be reduced by improving building performance. Buildings have traditionally been designed as low performance, dur-

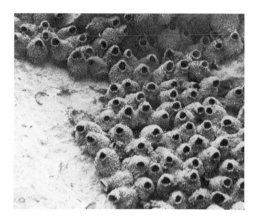

12. The nests of cliff swallows provides a parallel example of group form found in unselfconscious architecture.

able structures. An alternative strategy is to design them for high performance and short life. Buckminster Fuller delights in pointing out the inefficiency of buildings compared with other technological products:

'If you want to determine the degree of development of a building, just weigh it.' However, high performance is dependent on the availability of advanced technology materials, improved methods of structural analysis, and quality control. Efficient structural configurations possess a logic unrelated to user convenience. Unlike Fuller, Frei Otto displays great ingenuity in adapting his structural concepts to fit the human context. The structural component in most buildings is about one fifth, so that even quite significant advances in structural efficiency do not produce appreciable benefits. Greater savings of non-renewable resources could accrue from raising the efficiency of building services. In areas of high technological change, such as hospital and laboratory buildings, the expense of altering service feeds justifies the insertion of an intermediate layer of interstitial space (fig. 13)—given over entirely to services—between the live floors. The development of demountable building systems or a 'kit of parts' to permit new buildings to be 'cannibalized' from existing structures would facilitate recycling of resources. Rationalization of building codes could result in considerable material savings without any real loss of performance. As a strategy for resource conservation, upgrading building technology—understandable in a culture which places such a high value on technological achievement—is questionable if it increases society's dependence on complex, high energy industrial processes.

An alternative response is to upgrade humble materials such as industrial wastes, rubbish and earth. Hassan Fathy's classic experiment (1945–7) at Gourna (figs. 15, 16) illustrates the advantages of matching the architectural means with the task. Fathy set out to construct a new village for some seven thousand peasants at Gourna, opposite Luxor on the Nile River. He built the village out of traditional mud brick, employing an ancient method of building vaults without centring.

'An ordinary mud brick, dried in the sun, is perfectly adequate for building an ordinary house, and can in Egypt be made for next to nothing . . . the Engineer . . . thinks that the stronger a component is, the better it must be . . . *we must resist the temptation to improve on something that is already satisfactory*'.[8] (author's italics)

This is not the sort of technological elitism currently favoured; nevertheless, Fathy managed to build his houses for fourteen percent of the cost of alternative reinforced concrete structures. Technology does not necessarily provide superior ways of making buildings. What really matters is that the means selected should be appropriate to the task, otherwise technology is wasted.

The extreme durability of buildings means that they are often outflanked by the rapid rate of cultural and technological change. There are two strategies for coping with building obsolescence: planned obsolescence, or expendability, and a responsive, adaptable architecture. Expendability is a prime feature of exhibition design. Forty years after Mies' successful Deutscher Werkbund housing exhibition at Weissenhof (Stuttgart), Moshe Safdie put forward a similar idea for Expo '67. He proposed: 'A total urban structure housing two thousand families, and that the public and commercial areas be national exhibits. One country would take the school, another the medical clinic, a third the theater, all as *permanent* buildings. There would be none of the sacrilegious waste of building temporary pavilions and then demolishing them. All the structures would become part of the living community after and even during Expo'.[9]

As with consumer products such as cars and refrigerators, buildings can be designed with a pre-planned death rate. Rapid rates of social, economic and technological change suggest that buildings should be thought of as temporary, 'throw-away'

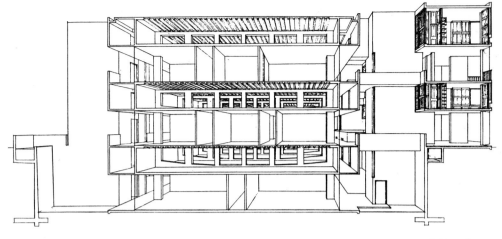

13. The expression of engineering services monumentalized in the Richards Building (p. 38) was validated by Louis Kahn with the introduction of intermediate floors in the Salk Institute at San Diego, California, in 1965, which were given over to the laboratory's intestines.

structures. Archigram in particular was drawn by the opportunity to scandalize the English architectural establishment with slogans of expendability. One of the perils of planned obsolescence is premature failure. The most serious objection, however, is that no nation could afford to replace its building stock every half century, or even a major portion of it. The wastage of resources resulting from planned architectural obsolescence is simply unacceptable in a world which is rapidly approaching the brink of resource exhaustion.

The alternative is an architecture capable of random adaptations in response to changing patterns of use. The Japanese Metabolist group postulated a concept of architecture in which the durable components were isolated from others more susceptible to the pressures of change.

This strategy, it was proposed, would permit the architectural organism to renew its cells while maintaining continuity of life. The concept of building as an organism with a relatively permanent structure but capable of renewal with minimum disruption to its physical elements provides an ideal accommodation between the demands of change and economy.

The United States orbits about 140 million tons of various pollutants into the atmosphere annually (fig. 14), or about three-quarters of a ton per person, per year. Most people do not need to be reminded of pollution, they already experience it! Nevertheless, a 1968 UNESCO conference concluded that man had about twenty years before the planet started to become uninhabitable on grounds of air pollution alone. The Swiss marine research scientist, Professor Jacques Piccard, predicts that all life in the sea will be dead within twenty-five to thirty years.

Reyner Banham has traced the relationship between nineteenth-century industrial pollution and the improvization of mechanical services to ameliorate conditions inside buildings. It is likely that as the earth's environment becomes increasingly inimical to organic life, buildings will come to resemble submarines and spacecraft by the deployment of air-locks, decontamination rooms and self-sustaining life support systems. They will serve as islands of health and well-being, surrounded by an ill-tempered environment. Two third-generation buildings provide an intimation of the consequences of such an architectural introversion. John Andrews designed Scarborough College (fig. 17) to ward off the harsh Canadian winter; not poisonous, but definitely uncomfortable. The building aligns itself along a multi-storey interior street, sheltering the life of its large college community within a monolithic body. Kevin Roche gave his Ford Foundation Headquarters Building (fig. 18) on Manhattan Island natural lungs, by enclosing a small forest behind the building skin.

World population is growing by 70 million people every year. It is anticipated that world population, numbered at 3,551 million in mid-1969, will double in the next

14. Skyscrapers thrust snorkel-like above the fetid air of Manhattan Island.

thirty-five to thirty-seven years. The medium United Nations forecast, issued in 1963, projected a world population of about 6130 million in the year 2000. This runaway population is already making unprecedented demands on its environment. The storm has been long a-building. There have been three significant surges of population growth sponsored by the cultural, agricultural and industrial-medical revolutions. It took about ten thousand years for world population to climb from 5 million to 500 million in 1650 A.D. Since then, there has been a progressive reduction in the time required for population to double, from two hundred years (1850), to eighty years (1930), and then to forty years (1970). Present population is the work of three major demographic trends. The industrialization of western countries was accompanied by a decline in the death rate. This was reflected by rapid population growth. After a time, the industrialized countries entered a period of demographic transition which was characterized by a decline in the birth rate and the population growth rate of these countries fell below the world average. The third major demographic trend appeared about the time of the Second World War, namely the dramatic decline in the death rate in the underdeveloped countries subsequent to the widespread diffusion of modern medical technology. Out of the estimated increase in world population by 2000, underdeveloped countries will contribute 2179 million and the developed countries 359 million (medium forecast). The pollution and natural resource load placed on the world environmental system by each person in an advanced country is possibly ten to twenty times greater than the load generated by a person in an underdeveloped country. Although the developed countries' share in population growth is only about one-sixth of the underdeveloped regions, the impact of this smaller population on the world environment will be substantially greater. Unless there is a massive increase in the death rate, rapid population growth will continue for the next 30 years, even taking into consideration a drastic reduction in the birth rate. This is because 'thirty-seven percent of the world's population are under 15, and those young people are going to have children and grandchildren before they move from the 0–15 age group to the 50–65 age group and start dying of old age'.[10]

The heat of accelerating population growth has been captured by the universal expansion of metropolises. The successive concentration of people in cities reinforced the dominance of urban over rural interests. In 1970 more than seventy percent of the population of the United States lived in cities, and this is fairly typical of other developed countries. The underdeveloped countries participated in this urbanizing trend with a fifty-five percent increase between 1950 and 1960. Two conditions are of special interest to the architect and planner, the effects of crowding and stress and the loss of freedom attending the 'slavery of large numbers'.

Until recently, biologists thought that Malthusian 'misery' imposed the ultimate natural limit on the growth of populations. In his celebrated study of the die-off of Sika deer on James Island in 1958, John Christian showed that stress induced by overcrowding—and not predators, starvation or disease—was the decisive factor in the massive population collapse. He found that as the numbers of animals in a given area increase, stress builds up until it triggers an endocrine reaction that acts to collapse the population. It is worth noting that the human pituiary adrenal system responds under stress in a way similar to other mammals. There is indirect evidence to show that inmates of concentration camps experienced acute forms of the stress syndrome that may have accounted for many deaths. Hoagland Hudson concluded that in all cases experimentally investigated 'the mortality is found to be dependent on population density and to cease below a certain critical population density'.[11] A further investigation of wood-chuck populations by Christian revealed that dominant individuals are less susceptible to stress. Following on from Christian's conclusions,

15. Hassan Fathy, plan of the new Gourna Village.
16. A typical mud brick house in the new Gourna Village near Luxor in Upper Egypt, as built by Hassan Fathy.

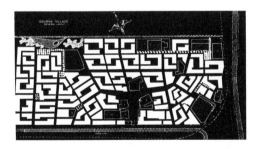

17. Scarborough College provides an environmental shield against the Canadian winter. Architect: John Andrews.

18. An interior terraced garden serves as the lungs for Kevin Roche's Ford Foundation Headquarters Building on Manhattan Island.

John Calhoun devised a series of experiments with controlled populations of Norway rats to determine the effects of the social behaviour of a species on population growth and of population density on social behaviour (fig. 19). His experiments produced an abundance of observations, some of which may have some reference to problems of human behaviour. The connection between crowding and pathological behaviour depends on the effect crowding has on disrupting important social functions leading to social disorganization. Calhoun observed disruptions of nest building, sex behaviour, reproduction and social behaviour, accompanied by serious physiological effects. The study of animal behaviour and populations, admittedly of limited relevance to the human condition, has aroused biologists such as Desmond Morris to the dangers inherent in the present uncontrolled growth of human numbers and intensive urbanization. 'Optimism is expressed by some who feel that since we have evolved a high level of intelligence and a strong inventive urge, we shall be able to twist any situation to our advantage; that we can re-mould our way of life to fit any of the new demands made by our rapidly rising species-status. That when the time comes, we shall manage to cope with the overcrowding, the stress, the loss of privacy and the independence of action; that we shall remodel our behaviour patterns and live like ants; that we shall control our aggressive and territorial feelings, our sexual impulses, and our parental tendencies; that if we have to become battery chicken-apes, we can do it; that our intelligence can dominate all our basic biological urges. I submit that this is rubbish.'[12] The architect and planner can alleviate the stress of crowding by ensuring the adequate provision of individual territories and privacy for families (figs. 20, 21).

The need to build for man, to subordinate bureaucratic planning and technological processes to the goal of a varied and flexible adjustment of the built environment to the individual became a much abused catch-phrase in the sixties. A number of people, including Kikutake, Kurokawa, Alexander and Archigram proposed the separation of communal and private responsibilities. The clearest exposition of this point of view came from Nicholas Habraken. Habraken reasoned that the individual dweller could regain the freedom to decide on the arrangement of his dwelling if mass housing was articulated into two distinct entities, supports and detachable units. He defined supports as permanent service structures, constructed and maintained by the community. In Habraken's scheme, the individual dweller selects from an array of

19. The growth of the world population. Unit: 100 million persons.

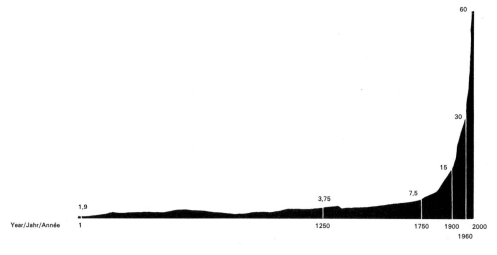

mass-produced, standardized detachable units, a set which most closely fits his needs, and instals it in an appropriate support structure. It is doubtful whether the detachable units will amount to a substantial enough proportion of the total structure to warrant extensive industrialization of building. The significance of Habraken's proposal arises from his articulation of the public and private spheres as a way of easing the constriction of individual freedom. This strategy is typical of much third-generation theory.

Lewis Mumford concluded *Technics and Civilization* in 1933 with an appeal for the establishment of dynamic equilibrium. He proclaimed that '. . . dynamic equilibrium, not indefinite progress, is the mark of the opening age; balance, not rapid one-sided advance; conservation, not reckless pillage.'[13] Mumford emphasized the necessity for equilibrium in the environment, equilibrium in industry and agriculture, and equilibrium in population. The sort of stability envisaged does not imply a stultifying transfixation of life; rather, it accepts the need for change and adjustment guided by a just appraisal of the natural limits of world ecology and resources. The greatest challenge now is how to handle the transition from growth to equilibrium. The controlled reduction of pollution and population are frequently presented as the way to avoid present dangers. Using models of the world system based on feedback-loop dynamics, Jay Forrester and his team at the Massachusetts Institute of Technology were able to represent the interactions between world population, industrialization, depletion of natural resources, agriculture and pollution. This investigation shows that periods of transition are accompanied by severe stress. Pressures must rise far enough to suppress the forces that produce growth.

Assuming technology frees the industrial system from its dependence on natural resources (fig. 22), population rises to a peak and then declines because of a pollution crisis. If, however, capital accumulation is increased and the 'normal' birthrate is reduced fifty percent, capital investment continues to grow until the pollution crisis develops (fig. 23). After an initial decline, population is again pushed up by a rapid rise in the quality of life that precedes the collapse. Success in reducing the pollution load (fifty percent) in company with an increased capital investment rate and reduced natural resource usage (fig. 24) delays the pollution crisis by twenty years and allows population to grow twenty-five percent further. Actions at one point in the system which attempt to relieve one type of distress produce an unexpected result in some other part of the system. One set of conditions that establishes a world equilibrium (fig. 25) requires the following reductions: capital investment, forty percent; birth rate, fifty percent; pollution generation, fifty percent; natural resource usage, seventy-five percent; and food production, twenty percent. The

20, 21. Terraced flats in Stuttgart, Germany. Architects: Faller & Schröder, with Reinhold Layer.

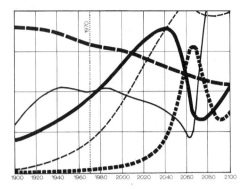

22. Natural resources depletion rate reduced by 50 percent below 1970 levels.

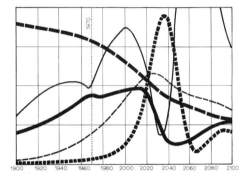

23. Capital accumulation increased by 20 percent, birth rate reduced 50 percent.

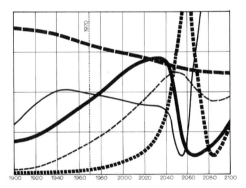

24. 20 percent increase of capital investment, 75 percent reduction of natural resource usage, birth rate reduced 50 percent.

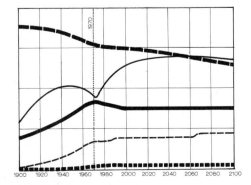

reduction in capital investment and suppression of food production would appear to be anti-humanitarian; nevertheless, if Forrester's calculations are reliable, merely suppressing population, pollution and resource depletion alone will not stabilize the world system.

The Danish physicist, Niels Bohr, taught:

'The opposite of a correct statement is a false statement. But the opposite of a profound truth may well be another profound truth.'[14]

Wright's formulation of an organic architecture as a sort of spiritual harmony binding man, architecture and nature in a whole, contains a profound truth which was countered by the rational-machine architecture created by the Europeans in the twenties. One of the gravitational drives of the third generation was to reconcile these two opposite statements and invent a composite view which accepted the machine as the legitimate tool of production, but asserted the primacy of man and nature over the needs of machinery. This pervasive impulse is strongly evident in the work of Utzon and Safdie. The organic principle exercises a stronger attraction for Utzon, whereas Safdie is drawn to the machine. But although they strike a different balance, their ultimate concern is to combine the assets of both. Christopher Alexander, peremptorily a rationalist, appears to be heavily committed to creating a theoretical framework for negotiating an agreement setting out the terms for the establishment of a state of psychic wholeness with the environment. To a greater or lesser extent, the struggle between these two opposite and profound truths—the organic and rational-machine principles—is apparent throughout the work of the third generation architects. Each individual strikes a balance according to his temperament and cultural situation. The assertion of organic wholeness provides a practical programme and spiritual ideal for subduing the rampant forces now rending the environment. It is a necessary preliminary to the institution of dynamic balance.

25. One set of conditions that establishes a world equilibrium: 1970 capital investment rate reduced 40 percent, birth rate reduced 50 percent, pollution generation reduced 50 percent, natural resource usage reduced 75 percent, and food production reduced 20 percent.

■ ■ ■ ■ ■ ■  Natural resources
———————  Quality of life
▬▬▬▬▬▬  Population
--------------  Capital investment
■■■■■■■■■  Pollution

## Chapter 2 · Pattern Language

Man thinks in a language. Benjamin Lee Whorf's study of the language of the Hopi Indians of Northern Arizona led him to conclude that being a neutral medium, language actually played a decisive role in shaping man's experience of the real world. He asserted that to a large extent the house of man's consciousness is built up on the language habit of the group. Each language is unique. It is effectively a vast pattern system which filters reality; it is characteristic of a language that it notices and neglects certain types of relationships and phenomena.

Patterns of thought are controlled by the unconscious systematizations of language. Unlike Whorf, Wilhelm von Humboldt saw the unique patterns of language as projecting the intricate structures of the mind: '*By the same process, whereby he spins language out of his own being, he ensnares himself in it;* and each language draws a magic circle round the people to which it belongs, a circle from which there is no escape save by stepping out into antoher'.[15] (author's italics)

Just as thought is formulated through the medium of language, so, too, the creation of physical forms is dependent on mental images or protoforms. It is the nature and relationship of these mental images which determines the quality of built form. Christopher Alexander suggests that '. . . every environment gets its morphology from millions of personal acts made by its builders, and these acts are themselves guided exclusively by the combination of the images which the builders already have in their heads at the time of the act'.[16] The underlying similarity between language and these images derives from the observation that both serve as a generator of form. Language arbitrates between reality and thought. Pattern language provides the vital connection between context and form creation; 'when we examine these combinatorial systems of images closely, we find that they are exactly like human languages. *Both are systems which allow a person to produce an infinite variety of unique combinations by means of his own creative act. For this reason, I call these systems pattern languages*'.[17] (author's italics)

Pattern languages are built up of patterns. These patterns are simply mental images which we select in order to create form. Psychologists call these mental images schemata. Bundles of related schemata are termed schema. Those schemata we employ to repeat existing forms are referred to as reproductive schemata. Thus pattern languages are really a kit of parts which man uses in shaping his environment. The rules governing the relationship of the units of language or pattern are its grammar. The vocabulary and grammar of pattern languages varies enormously from culture to culture. In primitive cultures, pattern languages tend to be simple, homogenous and relatively static. In more complex cultures, pattern languages exhibit stages of growth and evolution similar to organic life cycles. The clarity, simplicity and meaning characteristic of static pattern languages tend to be lost in the search for breadth and refinement of expression. In highly complex and mobile cultures such as our own, a number of pattern language systems co-exist and overlap, but there is considerable confusion between their boundaries. The profusion of separate, personal pattern languages and their lack of correspondence with reality is at the source of the crisis in contemporary form.

The basic unit of pattern language is the schemata. An English psychologist, Terence E. Lee, has carried out extensive explorations into the nature of man's mental images of his environment. According to Lee: 'A socio-spatial schema is built up as a "model in the head" from the continuous input that comes from the billions of transactions with the external world. Each new experience is sorted into all the schemata to which it may have some relevance. It is assimilated, and in the process changes the schema but then it is finished in its original form. It is the continuously changing schemata that are stored and which serve as a framework for future behaviour in the environment.

We each build up a large number of such socio-spatial schemata during a lifetime and their content depends on our experience. We all have, for example, a body schema, a home, street, neighbourhood and city schema, and none of them corresponds exactly to "reality" as measured by Euclidean geometry.'[18]

Our spatial schemata are mental structures which have become organized for particular purposes. They are the space we inhabit, and the images are selected in order to create form. Those schemata which we employ directly as templates for creating form are known as reproductive schemata. They are the same as Christopher Alexander's patterns. Norberg-Schulz defines schemata as 'habits of perception which have become established in such a way that they acquire the character of quasi-objects'. He notes that '*reproduction only considers those elements in perception which fit the reproductive schemata*, and must conclude that we neither reproduce what we see nor what we are able to see, *but what our reproductive schemata make possible*'.[19] (author's italics)

In spite of their general inaccessibility to observation, quite a lot is known about the constitution, structures and functions of schema. The remainder of this chapter is devoted to describing the character of reproductive schemata, their associations into languages and the implications that all this has for the form-making process.

We have already noted the divergence between perception and reality. A similar discrepancy exists between schema and reality as measured by Euclidean geometry. Craig and Koestler argue that the main function of the nervous system is to model or parallel external events. Both Jencks and Alexander make the point that our schema actually come in contact with reality when they definitely fail to correspond. Otherwise, the formation and refinement of schema follows a cyclical process of hypothesis and correction. The more we concentrate, the closer the correspondence between our schema and reality. Never at any stage of the process can it be said that the schema is identical to reality. This fact has profound implications for pattern language. The forms man makes never exactly correspond to their context. The divergence between form and context, the extent of the misfit, is determined to a considerable degree by the appropriateness of the pattern language employed. The more appropriate the pattern language, the more successful will be the resultant form in terms of the needs it was intended to meet.

The content as opposed to the form of our schema is constantly being changed and refined by interaction with the environment. Confirmation of the cumulative nature of schema building can be demonstrated by returning to an urban environment made familiar in childhood and matching the old schema with the new information. Norberg-Schulz has observed that 'any new situation demands a certain revision to the schemata, and an active relation to the environment presupposes such flexibility'.[20]

There are two basic types of pattern language. In static pattern languages, neither the constituent patterns nor the structural relationship of the patterns is modified significantly. Such languages persist for millennia without any significant re-shaping of the language. They are associated with cultures in which the form-making process is largely unselfconscious (fig. 1). The pattern languages used in complex, highly developed civilizations are usually living languages. In such pattern languages the essential forms may remain relatively unchanged. The constituent patterns undergo extensive modification in response to changes in the environment. Indeed, some pattern languages such as that evolved by the culture of classical Greece demonstrate enormous survival powers. Far from following a restricted cycle of gestation, youth, maturity and decadence, they leapfrog from one civilization to another.

1. The environmental structure of the Neolithic town of Catal Hüyük in Anatolia is an early prototype of unselfconscious form-making.

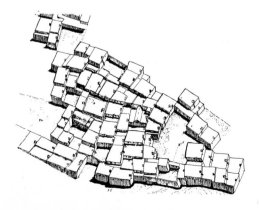

2. A quality of unity and inclusive integration pervades the Trulli village form of Southern Italy.

The wholeness of a pattern language is usually assessed in terms of the environmental structure it promotes. When the structure of the man-made environment is seen as an integrated picture of the way of life of a people, it is said to be whole. It may be inferred that the pattern language used for generating this environmental form also possesses a quality of unity and inclusive integration. Whole pattern languages frequently occur in association whith relatively primitive cultures (fig. 2). As a culture becomes more complex and subject to change, the pattern languages it uses need to be more acutely differentiated and flexible. Thus, complexity, specialization and rapid cultural change mitigate against the formation of inclusive whole pattern languages, whose formation out of the raw material of experience is a slow process. The inherent inertia of pattern languages ensures that in rapidly changing cultures such as our own, their terms always fail to match the realities of the present.

It is impossible to discuss pattern language in isolation from the form-making process. There are as many pattern languages as there are variations of the process. Pattern languages are generated by the need to shape form, and to a large extent their composition and organization is tailored to fit the particular requirements of each cultural context. We may discern two basic types of form making. In unselfconscious cultures, form-making is learned informally through imitation and correction. Form follows tradition. Buildings are not designed, they are simply constructed according to a common formula which is repeated over and over again. In order to learn form-making, people need only learn to repeat the patterns of tradition. The distinction between unselfconscious and selfconscious cultures depends on whether forms are designed by specialists or created by the people who use them. This definition is not as arbitrary as it might appear, because the latter usually prevail in primitive folk cultures. In selfconscious cultures, form-making is taught in special schools, according to explicit rules. In unselfconscious cultures the identification of the context $C_1$ with the appropriate schema $C_2$ and its matching with the reproductive schema $F_2$ is governed by habit (fig. 3). The actual shaping of the form $F_1$ and its matching with the relevant reproductive schema $F_2$ involves an active interaction between the two (fig. 4). The form-making process in selfconscious cultures provides a number of illuminating contrasts. Here, the variety and complexity of needs for which forms are required is vastly greater. The definition of the context and the assembly of schemata which accurately describe it presupposes an active interaction between the designer and the context, and the number of reproductive schema he has at his disposal is usually correspondingly enlarged. Hence the conceptual interaction between the concept of the context (schema $C_2$) which the designer has learned or invented and the reproductive schemata or mental templates for the new form which are infinitely more complex. Once the reproductive schemata have been finalized, their transposition into form is governed by fairly rigid rules. These ensure that the resultant form precisely matches the mental prototype. The pattern languages employed for form-making in unselfconscious and selfconscious cultures vary enormously.

In so many ways the forms of unselfconscious cultures are the antithesis of our own environment. In such cultures the forms are saturated with meaning. The village form is a symbol system which mirrors man's image of himself and the universe. The pattern of forms is a picture of the culture, embodying a way of life which is coherent and whole. In the process, these forms acquire a clarity of meaning which is compellingly real. Moreover, their very responsiveness to life and the land ensures a quality of rightness which seems eternally valid. They succeed almost effortlessly where modern architects have failed so laboriously in finding the right forms. They have no need of an intellectual functionalism, for function is a way of life, a means of survival.

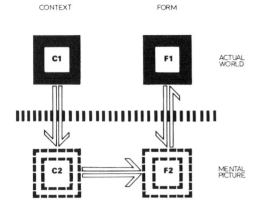

3. Schematic diagram of unselfconscious form making.

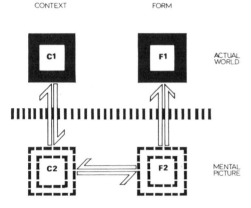

4. Schematic diagram of selfconscious form making. Key: C1 context, C2 schemata, F2 reproductive schemata, F1 form.

5. The unsuitability of the Japanese raised-floor dwelling in winter is explained by its derivation from the Ise shrine prototype.

The extreme fitness of forms produced by unselfconscious cultures has long been appreciated. Frank Lloyd Wright was probably the first modern architect to recognize their significance:

'That is why folk building growing in response to actual needs, fitted into environment by people who knew no better than to fit them to it with native feeling . . . are today for us better worth study than all the highly selfconscious academic attempts at the beautiful throughout all Europe.'[21] In his introduction to *Architecture without Architects*, Bernard Rudofsky claims that 'the shapes of houses, sometimes transmitted through a hundred generations, seem eternally valid, like those of "their tools"'.[22]

The ability of unselfconscious cultures to produce forms which fit their context and achieve a clarity of organization is the major theme running through Alexander's analysis of the form-making process. The directness of response to misfits in unselfconscious cultures means that each failure is corrected soon after it occurs. In direct contrast to this responsiveness, tradition, taboo and myth act as shock absorbers, dampening the impact of each misfit and localizing its influence. The effect of rigid tradition is to hold the whole pattern system steady while permitting minor adjustments to be made as they are needed. It is this combination of directness of response and rigid tradition which renders the forms self-adjusting.

It is evident that the secret of the success of unselfconscious cultures depends on two factors, possession of a valid pattern language and stability of the culture. The choice of the raised floor dwelling by the ancient Japanese aristocracy as the prototype for their dwellings provides a unique example of the consequences arising from the adoption of an unsatisfactory pattern language (fig. 5). Because the raised floor dwelling was basically unsound in terms of the Japanese winter, adjustments and corrections were made to the life style of the aristocracy.

The Slovakian peasant shawlmakers cited by Alexander provide an example of what happens when a successful tradition is interrupted. The advent of analine dyes made available a greater variety of colours, and this in turn disrupted the rigid formulae which had previously enabled the Slovakian peasants to make beautiful shawls. It is well known that if an unselfconscious culture undergoes radical changes which invalidate fundamental aspects of the pattern language, it is universally unable to invent new successful pattern languages.

How have unselfconscious cultures come by such excellent pattern languages? Evolution may contain in part an answer to the problem. The integration of multiple levels of human experience into whole coherent pattern languages suggests that they developed over a long period of time. Richness of meaning was rubbed off on the forms by their exposure to life. Just as in biology the fit members of a species are relatively more successful, so too, it is possible that the chance discovery of fit patterns assisted the survival of human groups. The growth of pattern languages occurred very slowly and painfully, which in part explains their extreme durability and the persistence of tradition. In the past, pattern languages were not invented, but evolved out of the process of life.

In unselfconscious cultures, it is the relationship of form to cultural systems which has elicited the deepest response among modern architects. The forms of unselfconscious culture are saturated with meaning. The total experience of life in all its multiplicity and layers of meaning has been integrated into simple coherent pattern languages. The accommodation of complexity and contradiction within the village form gives it richness. The community of form provides a picture of the culture (fig. 6). The village is a symbol system which mirrors man's image of the universe, and the relationship of the dwellings describes the social order of the makers.

Aldo van Eyck was deeply impressed by the integration of life and form among the

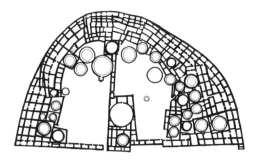

6. The distinctive pattern of cylindrical kivas and cells provides a picture of the culture sheltered within the Pueblo Bonito in Chaco Canyon.

7. The integration of life with form by Dogon tribesmen. Gogoli, and the market place in Ogol.
8. An aerial view of Logone-Birni, Cameroun, reveals the repetition of a simple vocabulary of forms which generates a unique pattern language.

Dogon tribesmen (fig. 7). Again and again in his writings on the Dogon, van Eyck reiterates that every 'artifact—whether small or large, basket or city, was identified with the universe or the power of the deity representing the cosmic order'.[23] Elsewhere he suggests that their behaviour is motivated by the need to feel at home in the universe. By refashioning his habitat in his own image, man makes form comprehensible, familiar and meaningful. Aldo van Eyck is supported by Bernard Rudofsky's observation that 'above all it is the humaneness of this architecture that ought to bring forth some response in us'.[24]

It seems that primitive man does not distinguish between different types of symbol-systems, but merges them all into magic and myth. This is especially true in the East where the urban form reflected a cosmic order. In the Japanese capital cities of Nara and Kyoto, urban space was structured 'by the exact arrangement of built symbols which, through their height, volume and outstanding overall shape produced a microcosmic image of a macrocosmic conception—a reflection of the whole world order to a smaller scale, a town scale, the reflection being the current man's deep understanding of the secrets of the cosmos'.[25]

It is apparent that many unselfconscious cultures owe their success as form-makers to the possession of a single inclusive pattern language. All the forms which collectively make up their environment are related in some way. Commenting on the Mousgoum huts built by African tribesmen of the French Cameroun (fig. 8), Alexander suggests that 'even superficial examination shows that they are all versions of the same single form type'.[26] The same idea is expressed by Aldo van Eyck: 'It seems to me that people for whom *all things are so much one thing, that one thing can be all things, carry this essential unity within themselves*'.[27] (author's italics) (fig. 9)

It is characteristic of buildings by unselfconscious cultures that one material predominates. This assists measurably in unifying the forms. The industrial age made a multiplicity of materials available to designers, and much of the ugliness of our present environment is attributable to their unrestrained use. The conscious decision to limit the range of materials employed in a building, known as 'mono-material', has been widely appreciated and applied with considerable success in establishing wholeness of form. Nevertheless, the concept of mono-material imposes an unreal simplicity, and so avoids the challenge of complexity.

The transition from an unselfconscious to a selfconscious situation involves a great many subtle transformations in pattern language. The first thing one notes is that with the advent of complex urban cultures, pattern languages become more specialized. In Greek and Egyptian civilizations, form-makers used at least two discernible pattern languages. The old unselfconscious pattern language was preserved in the dwellings of the peasantry and new pattern languages evolved parallel to them for housing the institutions created by the new civilization. The designers of the new temples and public buildings worked within the rules of a tradition, modifying and adjusting the basic pattern ever so slightly. The new pattern languages of civilization may be distinguished from those of unselfconscious cultures by the fact that they are subject to change and growth. They are living languages, and the boundaries between the pattern language systems are clearly defined.

Pattern languages became more specialized. At a much later date the boundaries between different pattern systems began to break down. The co-existence of multiple overlapping pattern languages greatly complicates the designer's task, because the range of reproductive schema increases correspondingly. The freedom flowing from this situation is to some extent counter-balanced by the opportunities for mis-matching the reproductive schema.

Pattern languages require time to achieve equilibrium every time a misfit occurs. When the rate of cultural change outstrips the ability of a pattern language to adjust,

9. The sculptural unity and infinite variety of Mojacar hill town in the province of Almeria typifies unselfconscious architecture.

the number of misfits multiply, rendering it obsolete. For pattern languages to remain in contact with reality, the rate of cultural change must be sufficiently slow to permit the requisite adaptations to occur. It is apparent that the different systems within a culture change at different rates—some systems are able to change more rapidly than others.

Françoise Choay has pointed out that 'the acceleration of history reveals a vice inherent in all built systems: a permanence and rigidity which make it impossible for them to continually transform themselves according to the rhythm set by the less rooted systems . . .'.[28]

Beyond a culture's threshold of adjustment, more rapid change results in the accumulation of unresolved problems. An accelerating rate of change such as has occurred over the past two centuries means that the problems have increased in number, complexity and difficulty while individual designers have less time to find answers.

The alignment of pattern language with reality in dynamic cultures follows repeated cycles of stability, incremental obsolescence and correction. As the correspondence between pattern language and reality breaks down under the pressure of cultural change, confidence in the language diminishes. The pace of cultural change in the twentieth century is such that: 'Each period requires a constituent language—an instrument with which to tackle the human problems posed bthe period, as well as those which from period to period remain the same.'[29]

Loss of confidence results in pattern instability. This in turn promotes wholesale experimentation with new and borrowed forms. The random and seemingly purposeless exploration of new ideas assists in the search for successful patterns which, properly integrated within the framework of the existing language, make possible the creation of a new order for the environment. When the extent and intensity of cultural change invalidate the foundations of its pattern language, such incremental corrections prove inadequate. In such circumstances, society needs to find a radically new order for structuring the environment. Clearly, elements of the older language system survive and are preserved within the new order.

Such a radical transformation affected European and American civilization during the nineteenth century and is still going on today. Form-makers sought to correct matters by the wholesale adoption of fossilized pattern languages from the past. Because the changes wrought by the advent of machinery were unprecedented, such fumblings were bound to fail. What was needed was a new pattern language. In *Theory and Design in the First Machine Age*, Reyner Banham provides a detailed account of the search for a modern pattern language. He shows that the machine aesthetic which emerged in the nineteen-twenties was not entirely new; it simply renewed the old ideas of the academy. It is clear that faced with the challenge of inventing a new pattern language, the designer reinterprets tradition. It is not possible to invent something as complex as a pattern language.

Much has been written about the origins and development of the modern movement in architecture. The following discussion attempts to describe the essential features of its pattern language. The machine aesthetic which appeared during the late nineteen-twenties was based on an analogy with machine production. In the absence of a genuinely industrialized building industry, the architects of the twenties created an architectural language which mimed selected features of machine production. They accepted machine technology 'without having bothered to acquaint themselves with it very closely'. Reyner Banham concludes 'that they produced a Machine Age architecture only in the sense that its monuments were built in a Machine Age, and expressed an attitude to machinery—in the sense that one might stand on French soil and discuss French politics, and still be speaking English'.[30]

With the appearance of large industrialized building programmes after the Second World War, the aesthetic language of modern architecture was found to be largely irrelevant. The correspondence between the pattern language of modern architecture and the reality of machine production was slight. The generations of architects who followed were faced with the task of remaking modern architecture in the workshop and factory. Many found it easier to jettison the machine aesthetic and become technologists.

If it is to create a whole environment, the pattern language used by its builders must be shared. Although modern architecture arose as an attempt to create buildings growing out of the actual conditions, it was expressed in a special form which made it inaccessible to all but a small band of initiates. Unlike the pattern languages of unselfconscious cultures which are shared by all members of the community, the language of modern architecture remained the exclusive property of architects. Many of the misunderstandings between architects and their clients occurred because the two used different pattern languages. Norberg-Schulz has pointed out that the non-architect's 'experience of architecture is based upon special schemata which consist of looking for the forms they are used to seeing . . . we may characterize these schemata as prejudices'.[31]

Unlike other specialists, the architect's use of a professional jargon affects everyone. We all share the environment. The machine aesthetic of the twenties was loaded with symbolic meanings derived from special conditions which prevailed at the time. This did not facilitate its general acceptance, even after much of the explicit symbolism had been discarded. The reaction against the international style in the late fifties produced a host of individual improvisations on the central theme, some so different and personal that they seemed to fall outside the meaning and intention of the mother language. The failure of modern architecture to achieve the status of a pattern vernacular for the environment has restricted its usage almost exclusively to architects.

The language of modern architecture was invented by a few sophisticated men out of the ideas of their time. Because it was distilled synthetically and did not arise organically out of the conditions of life, it lacked much of the richness and complexity of reality. Banham has commented that: 'in picking on the phileban solids and mathematics, the creators of the international style took a convenient short-cut to creating an ad-hoc language of symbolic forms, but it was a language which could only communicate under the special conditions of the twenties'.[32] (fig. 10)

Recognition of the narrowness of modern architecture has been slow in coming. In its early phase, modern architecture represented an artificial exclusive order which was incapable of encompassing the complexity and ambiguity of life. More often than not, modern architects sacrificed function for the sake of achieving clarity of form. In acknowledging the impossibility of solving all problems, Paul Rudolph claims that 'it is characteristic of the twentieth century that architects are highly selective in determining which problems they want to solve. Mies, for instance, makes wonderful buildings only because he ignores many aspects of a building. If he solved more problems, his buildings would be less potent'.[33]

It is probable that the tendency to eschew complexity and contradiction for the sake of clarity and order was dictated by the pattern language used. It requires time and contact with life for a pattern language to acquire the additional breadth and richness of meaning one associates with maturity. Many of the fads of the fifties were essential features of a difficult adolescence. The discovery of materials, structure, regionalism, climate and building services all assisted in extending the range and quality of its pattern vocabulary. Each significant building in the post-war era enriched the pattern language by adding to the total reservoir of reproductive schemata. The making of a pattern language is a continuous process. A language stops changing when it is in equilibrium. The task of the third generation was to include the realities of the situation with all their contradictions and confusions within the programme. To fail to do so was to risk separating architecture from life and the needs of society.

In the twenties, Le Corbusier and Mondrian turned to mathematics as a means of clarifying their methodologies. Forty years later, when architecture once again appeared to be outmanoeuvred by the rapidity of change then affecting the environment, architects returned to the prestige of mathematics to establish order out of chaos. One of the most important attempts to harness the logic of mathematics in the service of design came from a young architect-mathematician, Christopher Alexander. The original statement of his rationalized design method in *Notes on the Synthesis of Form* has since undergone a radical shift in emphasis. This may in part be attributed to experience gained by Alexander in the application of the theory to real problems. The establishment of the Center for Environmental Structure (CES) in March 1967 under a grant by Edgar J. Kaufmann enabled Alexander to test the

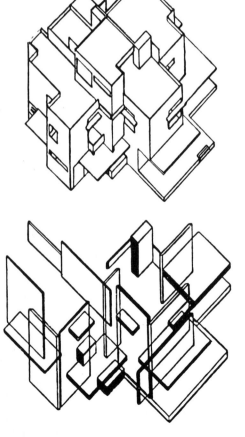

10. The first generation acquired an *ad hoc* language of symbolic forms. Theo van Doesburg and Cor van Eesteren, study for a house, 1923.

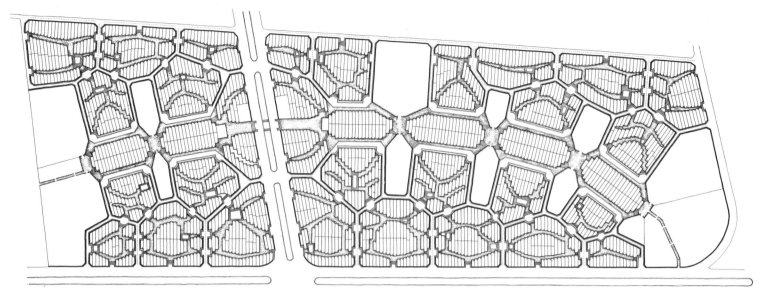

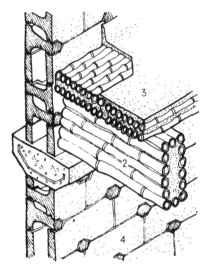

11–15. Low cost housing in Peru, United Nations project. Center for Environmental Structure, 1969.

11. A possible site arrangement employing the pattern language developed by the Christopher Alexander team.

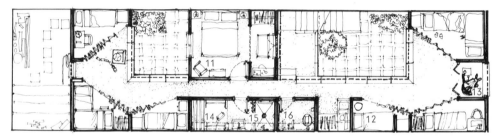

13. The generic house. Second floor.

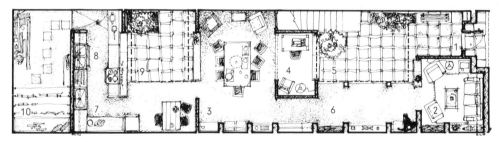

14. First floor. Key: 1 entrance, 2 sala (parlour), 3 family room, 4 family room alcove, 5 main patio, 6 veranda, 7 kitchen, 8 laundry, 9 kitchen patio, 10 storage patio, 11 master bedroom, 12 bed alcoves, 13 mirador, 14 clothes drying closet, 15 shower, 16 toilet.

15. The open section facilitates natural cross ventilation.

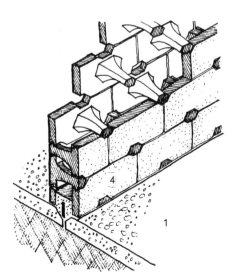

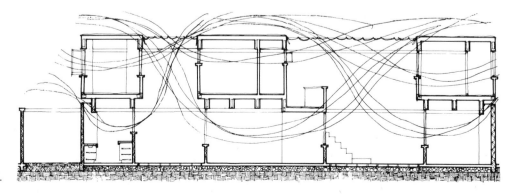

12. Construction method. Key: 1 floating slab, 2 bamboo-urethane foam beam, 3 bamboo-urethane foam plank, 4 mortarless block cavity wall.

theory in a number of pilot projects. The first of these was the design of a multi-service centre. Later, the Center collaborated with Skidmore, Owings and Merrill in the development of patterns for the South-West Regional Laboratory for Educational Research and Development. The Center's submission in the international competition sponsored by the United Nations for low-cost housing in Peru is perhaps the most conspicuously successful application of Alexander's pattern theory to date (fig. 11). The architectural proposals contained a description of the dwellers' social patterns loosely framed to ensure flexibility and adaptability to individual factors. The challenge of low cost elicited a number of ingenious constructional solutions.

In *Notes on the Synthesis of Form*, Alexander identifies the contemporary designer's inability to produce functional form with a failure to decompose the problem into its true components. Alexander quite rightly points out that the mesh of language tends to impose its own structure on the designer's analysis of the context. Thus, the designer mistakes the organization of his ideas, attributable to the impartiality of language, with the true structure of the problem. Alexander's solution is to use mathematics as a tool for identifying the problem's structure (figs. 12–15). The method is too complex to be adequately described here. The important thing is that the problem is broken down into related components or sets. These sets establish a foundation for the formulation of the patterns, which are then employed as form generators for synthesizing the whole form.

16. Diagram of interaction between Christopher Alexander's thirty-three requirements of housing.

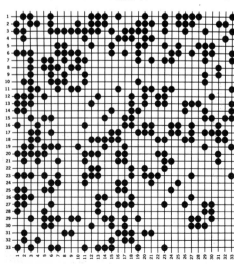

## The Basic Requirements of Dwelling

1 Efficient parking for owners and visitors; adequate manoeuvre space.

2 Temporary space for service and delivery vehicles.

3 Reception point to group. Sheltered delivery and waiting. Provision for information; mail, parcel, and delivery boxes; and storage of parcel carts.

4 Provision of space for maintenance and control of public utilities. Telephone, electricity, main water, sewerage, district heating, gas, air conditioning, incinerators.

5 Rest and conversation space. Children's play and supervision.

6 Private entry to dwelling, protected arrival, sheltered standing space, filter against carried dirt.

7 Congenial and ample private meeting space; washing facilities; storage for outdoor clothes and portable and wheeled objects.

8 Filters against smells, viruses, bacteria, dirt. Screens against flying insects, wind-blown dust, litter, soot, garbage.

9 Stops against crawling and climbing insects, vermin, reptiles, birds, mammals.

10 A one-way view of arriving visitors; a one-way visible access space.

11 Access points that can be securely barred.

12 Separation of children and pets from vehicles.

13 Separation of moving pedestrians from moving vehicles.

14 Protection of drivers during their transition between fast-moving traffic and the pedestrian world.

15 Arrangements to keep access clear of weather interference: overheating, wind, puddles, ice and snow.

16 Fire barriers.

17 Clear boundaries within the semi-private domain. Neighbour to neighbour; tenant to management.

18 Clear boundaries between the semi-private domain and the public domain.

19 Maintenance of adequate illumination, and absence of abrupt contrast.

20 Control at source of noises produced by servicing trucks, cars, and machinery.

21 Control at source of noises generated in the communal domain.

22 Arrangements to protect the dwelling from urban noise.

23 Arrangements to reduce urban background noise in the communal pedestrian domain.

24 Arrangements to protect the dwelling from local noise.

25 Arrangements to protect outdoor spaces from noise generated in nearby outdoor spaces.

26 Provision for unimpeded vehicular access at peak hours.

27 Provision for emergency access and escape, fire, ambulance, reconstruction, and repairs.

28 Pedestrian access from automobile to dwelling involving minimum possible distance and fatigue.

29 Pedestrian circulation without dangerous or confusing discontinuities in level or direction.

30 Safe and pleasant walking and wheeling surfaces.

31 Garbage collection point enclosed to prevent pollution of environment.

32 Efficient organization of service intake and distribution.

33 Partial weather control between automobile and dwelling.

In his early writings on pattern language, Alexander concentrated his attention on the analysis of the context. He provided detailed descriptions of the mathematical methods employed. Somewhat later, he seems to have appreciated along with 'all the king's horses and all the king's men', that taking things apart (decomposition) is one thing, and putting Humpty Dumpty back together again (synthesis) is considerably more difficult. The success of his method depends on the synthesis of the pattern elements into unified form. Aldo van Eyck has wryly commented: 'You cannot reach the other side without jumping—no arbitrary stop gap whim—team work or anti-prima donna nonsense—is going to bridge the gap. The art is in the jumping, how you take off, when and where. *Without the jump, there'll be no architecture—good or less good; just buildings and cities—bad or worse*'.[34] (author's italics)

Architectural thought in the sixties provides a number of interesting parallels with the twenties. In both periods the reaction against established ideals manifested itself in a rejection of aesthetic formulae. The anti-architecture philosophy of Gropius' collaborator, Hannes Meyer, finds its counterpart in such projects as Cedric Price's 'Thinkbelt'.

Towards the end of the fifties, modern architecture appeared to lose momentum. Archigram revived an attitude to architecture which had found its clearest expression in the earlier schemes of the Futurists. Both movements rejected aesthetic modes of design and substituted projections of the future based on technology. It is not so much the actual theories or ideas which suggest the parallel, as a common mood. Both eras display a deep discontent with the direction taken by architecture. They represent moments of discontinuity in tradition. Attempts to redefine the nature and responsibilities of architecture are immensely important. They are a necessary part of the process of realigning architecture with reality. The incremental adjustment and extension of the pattern language results in a closer parallel of form and context. To a great extent, the role of the third generation has been to reinterpret the meaning of modern architecture; to return to the grass roots. Reyner Banham's study of the sources of modern architecture in *Theory and Design in the First Machine Age* was symptomatic of the urge to rediscover modern architecture (fig. 17).

The rate of change in most advanced countries outran the architect's capacity to devise new solutions. The recognition of change as the only constant in the environment has profoundly affected contemporary consciousness. The search for new patterns is a precondition to re-establishing equilibrium.

New patterns were needed to enable designers to create the new forms. Many of the experimental schemes put forward by third generation architects are by nature ideograms (fig. 16). It is a mistake to consider them as practical detailed solutions to present problems. Many critics of the Metabolists and Archigram fail to observe this distinction. They ignore the Utopian proposals of the first generation which played such an important part in the formulation of the new architecture. These diagrams and proposals of the third generation constitute raw pattern material for reshaping and extending our contemporary pattern language. The product of this process is an expanded pattern language more closely attuned to present needs.

17. The two stage decomposition of the context into a program of sets must be matched with corresponding patterns and synthesized into a whole form.

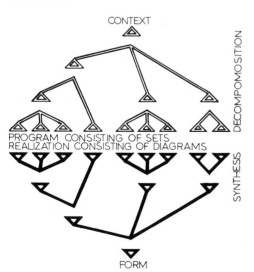

CONTEXT

DECOMPOMOSITION

PROGRAM CONSISTING OF SETS
REALIZATION CONSISTING OF DIAGRAMS

SYNTHESIS

FORM

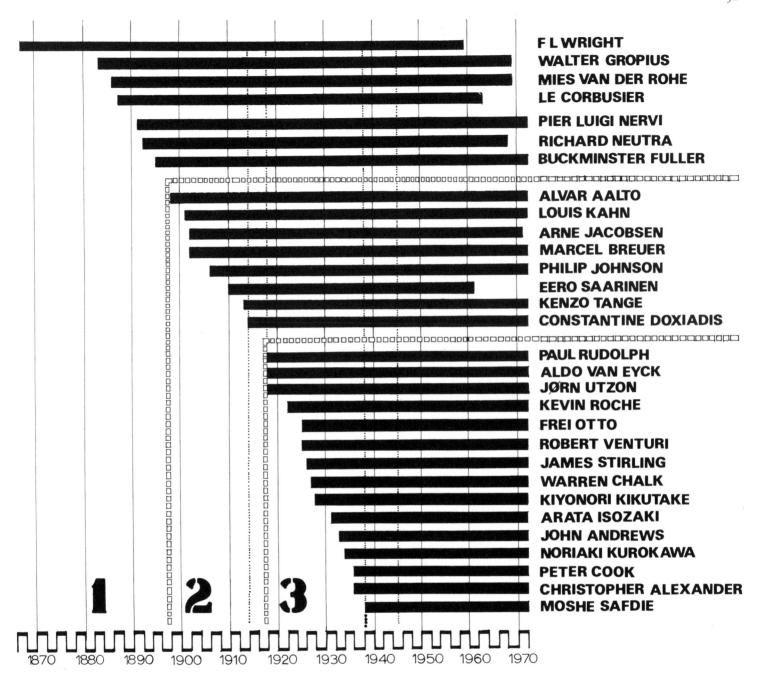

F L WRIGHT
WALTER GROPIUS
MIES VAN DER ROHE
LE CORBUSIER

PIER LUIGI NERVI
RICHARD NEUTRA
BUCKMINSTER FULLER

ALVAR AALTO
LOUIS KAHN
ARNE JACOBSEN
MARCEL BREUER
PHILIP JOHNSON
EERO SAARINEN
KENZO TANGE
CONSTANTINE DOXIADIS

PAUL RUDOLPH
ALDO VAN EYCK
JØRN UTZON
KEVIN ROCHE
FREI OTTO
ROBERT VENTURI
JAMES STIRLING
WARREN CHALK
KIYONORI KIKUTAKE
ARATA ISOZAKI
JOHN ANDREWS
NORIAKI KUROKAWA
PETER COOK
CHRISTOPHER ALEXANDER
MOSHE SAFDIE

**1  2  3**

1870  1880  1890  1900  1910  1920  1930  1940  1950  1960  1970

1. Although the boundaries defining each generation are vague, three generations of architects may be identified in the chronology of modern architecture. The third generation consists approximately of those individuals born in the inter-war period, 1918–38.

## Chapter 3 · The Third Generation

*'Each generation feels a new dissatisfaction and conceives a new idea of order.'*[35]

Peter and Alison Smithson, June 1955

*'The revolt of the third generation architects . . . is to secure an integrated human implementation of function and a richer formal language.'*[36]

Forrest Wilson, 1970

The real victor at the tenth congress of C.I.A.M. in 1956 was not Team 10 but Time. The first generation leadership of C.I.A.M. was then old. Le Corbusier was in his sixty-ninth year, and Gropius was four years his senior. Within a decade of the dissolution of C.I.A.M. at Otterlo, Wright, Corbu, Mies and Gropius were dead. The architects of the third generation were coming into their own.

The clash of ideas at Dubrovnik was evidence of a growing disenchantment among the younger architects with orthodox modern architecture. Two of the founding members of Team 10, Aldo van Eyck and Peter Smithson, led the attack on the establishment. They argued that in failing to realign itself with contemporary life, modern architecture had lost contact with reality. In effect, modern architects were building yesterday's dreams. They felt that the earlier interpretation of functionalism as mechanical was inadequate. Its meaning needed to be extended to include a whole range of environmental and human factors which up until then had either been ignored or merely hinted at. In essence, their criticism was that the rational architecture and Garden City movements had failed to provide an environment which accurately reflected their generation's idea of order.

Team 10 prepared the way for a comprehensive reappraisal of modern architecture, which entered a confused phase in which no idea, however sacred, remained unchallenged. The work of the third generation of modern architects is most easily viewed as a criticism of the first generation foundations, which was a necessary precursor to renewal of the movement.

The first generation were practical men. They knew that it was impossible with the limited resources at their disposal to solve all the problems at a stroke. If any real progress was to occur, it would be made by treating problems separately. Even a cursory study of their writings and architecture reveals a breadth and depth of perception. Many of the problems and ideas which now preoccupy the third generation were anticipated in the work of the first, who had tackled those problems which appeared to them most urgent. That we would now choose differently is no fault of theirs. The third generation takes for granted the great achievements of the first, responding to the problems which the master architects left unresolved. Mies, who was highly selective in the problems he tackled, observed that: 'The day will come when others who have something important to give will do what we would not do—architecture must develop out of the epoch, this was the way the old architecture developed. Each epoch did the most that it dared.'[37]

The third generation reacted against the tyranny of a too explicit functionalism. The elevation of functionalism from the status of a minor principle to a central dogma is relatively recent. Considerable confusion exists as to its meaning. Reyner Banham has pointed out that none of the major figures of the twenties were pure functionalists. Their work cannot be understood without reference to their aesthetic intentions. The architecture of the twenties was loaded with symbolic meanings, and it is apparent from Le Corbusier's writings that functional was interchangeable with

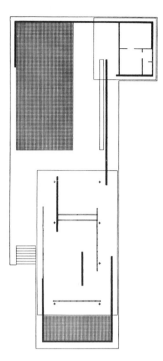

2. The celebration of rational clarity which Mies van der Rohe detected as the essence of his epoch was abstracted from a generalization of function expressed in the Barcelona Pavilion, 1929.

3. Antonio Sant'Elia's projection of future urban technology in his study of a Futurist City, 1914, affirmed his contention that architecture is synthesis and expression.

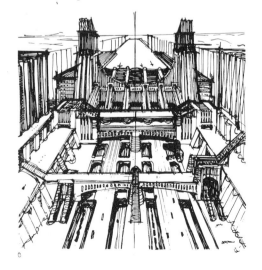

rational. In his view, it is the capacity of buildings to evoke a pleasurable response which entitles them to be given the name of architecture:

'But suddenly you touch my heart, you do me good, I am happy and I say this is beautiful. That is architecture. Art enters in.'[38]

Le Corbusier regarded individual expressionism as contrary to the spirit of the modern age. For Le Corbusier, aesthetics rather than function determined the form of his buildings. Mies van der Rohe was more equivocal: 'Our buildings can become worthy of the name of architecture only if they truly interpret their time by their perfect functional expression'.[39] If function has anything to do with economy, then Mies consistently subordinated it in his search for perfection. By his insistence that architecture interpret the time and express the essence of the epoch, Mies appears roughly in agreement with Le Corbusier.

Even Gropius, that staunch advocate of analysis and teamwork, appears in sympathy with the anti-functionalist mood of Le Corbusier. The Bauhaus did not enter its functionalist phase until Hannes Meyer took over from him. The prevalent outlook in the twenties accords very much with Sant'Elia's assertion 'that real architecture is not, for all that, an arid combination of practicality and utility, but remains art, that is synthesis and expression'.[40] (fig. 3)

The decline of German Expressionism after 1923 impoverished the formal language of modern architecture. The significance of Expressionism lies in its recognition of the irrational and emotional traits in human nature. The denial of irrational feeling in architectural design which paralleled the rise of the functionalist mystique was reinforced by events in the thirties. Many of the apologists of modern architecture arrived on the scene after the event and missed the symbolic meanings and associations which were so inextricably bound up with the formation of the new aesthetic. The new housing done in and around Berlin in the late twenties may have contributed to the myth of modern architecture as a cheap style.

The world depression and the rise of Fascism in Germany and Italy threatened the survival of modern architecture. In such desperate circumstances, it appeared more sensible to defend modern architecture on the grounds that it was rational and economical and to gloss over its symbolic and aesthetic connotations. The legend of modern architecture as functional and determinist was so firmly established by the nineteen-fifties that attempts to broaden its language were popularly considered to be a denial of fundamental principles. The necessary discipline of functionalism stripped modern architecture of additional richness of meaning which the third generation has sought to reinstate. However, the precedent of Expressionism and Futurism in the formative stages of modern architecture should dispel any doubts as to their legitimacy.

Functionalism embodies a disposition of mind typical of the post-medieval rationalist conception of the world. It arose out of a desire to impose a semblance of reasonableness on an essentially chaotic situation. Its justification lies not so much in history as in the need to impose a rational discipline on architecture. An aura of determinism surrounds the functionalists' demand that form follow function. Such features of the scientific outlook as determinism, the mechanical modelling of reality and the avoidance of phenomena which resist quantification are present in varying degrees in the functionalist argument. The dissatisfaction of the third generation with the basic creed of functionalism stems from an increasing doubt in this post-medieval conception of the world. The failure of technology to come to terms with man's humanity has called into question the intellectual framework of rationalism of which functionalism is a part.

Functionalism encouraged the articulation of compound problems according to the necessities of rational analysis. Translated into Corbusian terms, this meant: 'Archi-

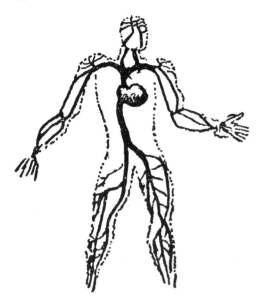

4. A biological form was used by Le Corbusier to support his decomposition of architectural problems into a simple hierarchy of separate elements.
5. The simple hierarchical systems of order crystallized in Le Corbusier's comparison of a tree with a tower block.

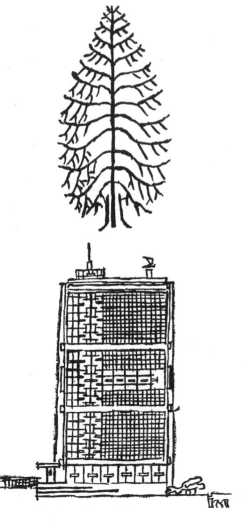

tecture, Town-planning, Determination of functions, Classification of functions, Hierarchy'.[41] It is evident from his equation of architecture and town-planning with 'impeccable biology'[42] (fig. 4) that the functional hierarchy Le Corbusier envisaged was that of a tree (fig. 5). By drawing attention to the tree structure, Le Corbusier crystallized the prevailing, though unconscious conception of physical order. Within this order, complex collective functions were reduced to associations of simple functions in a form which preserved the conceptual clarity of the analysis. It promoted the separate expression of structure, enclosure, services and programme functions. Mies' Barcelona Pavilion of 1929 (fig. 2) exploited with rigorous clarity the architectonic consequences of this attitude. By offsetting the cruciform columns from the walls, Mies clearly differentiated support and enclosure. The independence of the wall and roof elements served to emphasize their separate identities. Functionalism called into existence an entire system of detailing based on the aesthetic of articulating functions. The pursuit of separateness was promoted from an occasional diversion to a popular pastime by C.I.A.M.'s Athens Charter. In it, the major functional and circulation elements of the city were acknowledged by physically isolating one from another. C.I.A.M. recommended the separation of pedestrians from moving vehicles, work from housing, and recreation from everything else. Le Corbusier enjoined the separation of buildings from the ground.

The mania for sorting things into linguistic categories, and the extreme compartmentalization which resulted, sacrificed the ambiguity, multiplicity and richness of life. Christopher Alexander contends that the designer's tendency to reduce overlap and ambiguity by the substitution of tree for semi-lattice structures stems from the limited capacity of the human mind to form intuitively accessible structures of greater complexity. The living structure of the city is persistently conceived as a tree, because the mind's first response is to reduce ambiguity and overlap in a confusing situation. To this end, it is endowed with a basic intolerance of ambiguity.

Robert Venturi's gentle manifesto *Complexity and Contradiction in Architecture* reflects the general mood of the third generation. It brings together in one statement the entire spectrum of third generation concerns and beliefs. Venturi's vision of architecture is essentially poetic. It arises from a belief in life as complex and ironic. He pleads for an architecture enlivened by ambiguity and tension, and based on the recognition of the inherent limitations of systems of order.

Venturi stakes his architectural philosophy on the ultimate inconsistency of life. He associates the capacity to accept inconsistency with maturity. Confirmation of his view is instanced in a quotation from August Heckscher:

'The movement from a view of life as essentially simple and orderly to a view of life as complex and ironic is what every individual passes through in becoming mature . . . such inner peace as men gain must represent a tension among contradictions and uncertainties . . .'[43]

The Elizabethan poets hold a special place in Robert Venturi's argument. They achieved richness of meaning by exploiting the complexity and ambiguity of life. It is possible that the third generation's commitment to life on these terms is evidence that modern architecture has come of age. According to Venturi . . . 'a valid order accommodates the circumstantial contradictions of complex reality'.[44] By promoting the easy unity of exclusion, the first generation of modern architects risked separating architecture from life.

Both Venturi and Alexander reproach the first generation for insufficiently recognizing the limitations of their systems of order. Alexander's solution is to propose a more complex and flexible system based on the semi-lattice. In contrast, Robert Venturi suggests that meaning is enhanced by breaking the order. He instances Aalto, who appears to create order out of the inconsistencies (fig. 6).

The deployment of ambiguity in architecture affects both form and function. Modern architecture encouraged the separation and specialization of architectural elements as a source of functional efficiency. In practice, however, functional precision was thwarted by the indeterminacy of human behaviour. Noting this, architects and planners increasingly design environments as multi-functional. The case for functional ambiguity in school design is put by Hermann Hertzberger '. . . a thing exclusively made for one purpose, suppresses the individual because it tells him exactly how it is to be used . . . Therefore, a form must be interpretable—in the sense that it must be conditioned to play a changing role'.[45]

The interests of the third generation are so diverse and varied that no single criterion is sufficiently comprehensive to characterize their work. In the fifth edition of *Space, Time and Architecture*, Giedion included a list of attitudes which differentiate the third generation from developments in the twenties.

'The social orientation is pushed further: a more conscious regard for the anonymous client.

Open-ended planning: the incorporation of changing conditions as a positive element of the plan. Incorporation of traffic as a positive element of urban planning. Greater carefulness in handling the existing situation . . . an emphasis upon the architectural use of horizontal planes and different levels, more forceful use of artificial platforms as urbanistic elements.

A stronger relation to the past; not expressed in forms but in the sense of an inner relationship and desire for continuity. Further strengthening of sculptural tendencies in architecture . . . The right of expression above pure function.'[46]

This list provides a generalized image which broadly describes the architectural behaviour of the third generation. Jørn Utzon typifies the third generation for Giedion. Giedion's readiness to interpret an entire generation of concerns in terms of one individual undermines the objectivity of his account. He had seized upon Utzon because he alone among the third generation architects preserved a line of continuity and a balance between reason and feeling which coincided with this historian's prejudices. His account neglects the underlying responses and motives which give form to the third generation's thoughts.

The first generation's preoccupation with the machine and technology led them to neglect the human cause. The third generation rediscovered man. The reassertion of

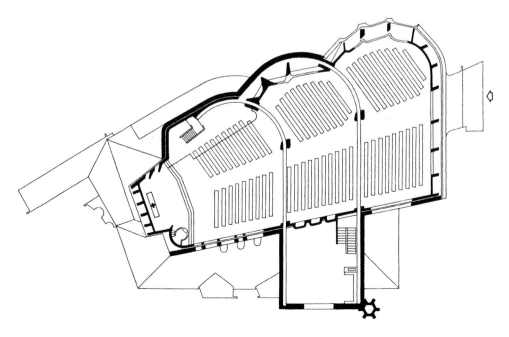

6. Alvar Aalto created order out of the contradictions of complex reality. Plan, Vuoksenniska Church, Imatra, Finland, 1956–9.

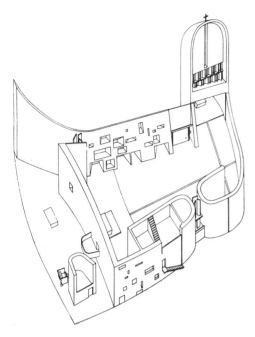

7. The Pilgrim's Church at Ronchamp precipitated the crisis of Rationalism. Architect: Le Corbusier, 1952.

architectural humanism generated a multiplicity of diverse responses. They may be summarized as acceptance of the irrational in human behaviour and rejection of rationalism; reassertion of the right of expression and rejection of the cult of genius; discovery of popular and anonymous form and the rejection of architectural authoritarianism; strengthening of organic form and the rejection of static, universal, exclusive systems of order; the affirmation of human worth and rejection of those aspects of functionalism which eliminated the human presence.

Le Corbusier precipitated the crisis of rationalism with his design of the Pilgrim's Church at Ronchamp (fig. 7). It challenged the entrenched supremacy of reason as the prime organizer of architectural form, and in so doing, decisively affected postwar development. Notre Dame du Haut is one of the most personal and potent buildings of its time. The early phases of modern architecture had resolved the balance of reason and feeling in architecture in favour of reason. Ronchamp reversed this preference. At Ronchamp, Le Corbusier turned his back on technological idealism and the machine aesthetic. He abandoned the rationalist ethic out of the need to register cultural ideas. He responded to the challenge of religious mysticism by creating an intensely sensuous architectural iconology.

A number of important third generation themes were initiated with Ronchamp: the strengthening of a sculptural tendency, and the reassertion of feeling in architecture and sensitivity to anonymous vernacular building. The superb relationship of architecture and landscape heralded a major philosophical re-orientation. The organic principle which had been suppressed in the early phase of modern architecture manifested itself in the work of Le Corbusier, Alvar Aalto and Jørn Utzon. Moshe Safdie and Jørn Utzon occupy a similar position because of their preference for an additive architecture based on group form and organized within the strict discipline of geometry.

The third generation brought together rational geometric and intuitive organic ideals in a dynamic synthesis. The architecture of Jørn Utzon, Moshe Safdie and the Japanese Metabolists exploits the tension and additional meaning engendered by the juxtaposition of these twin psychological polarities.

Form and expression were inextricably linked in Notre Dame du Haut. Architecture approached sculpture. The lifting of the prohibition against expression coincided with an increasingly sculptural interpretation of form, which became characteristic of third generation architecture. This study by Reyner Banham of Lou Kahn's Richards Laboratories stresses this (figs. 8,9). 'What it comes to is this: Kahn has dramatized the fact that his building is mechanically serviced, but he seems to be pretty insensitive to the nature of those services.'[47]

The other function of expression is to manifest meaning. Jørn Utzon's design for the Sydney Opera House evokes the essence of opera through the medium of abstract form much as Le Corbusier did at Ronchamp. The danger of permissive expression is that it frequently degenerates into arbitrary sensationalism or idiosyncratic forms which devalue architectural integrity.

Sigfried Giedion recognized an affinity between the third generation's conception of space and the first space conception in which 'space was brought into being by the interplay between volumes'.[48] Buildings such as Utzon's Sydney Opera House, Kikutake's Izumo Treasury and Reima Pietilä's Students' Union at Otaniemi (fig. 10) exhibit an awareness of 'the space-emanating qualities of free-standing buildings'[49] which Giedion identifies with the early space conception. In the beginning sculpture approached architecture, now architecture approaches sculpture. The third generation has continued the intermediate or hollowed-out interior space conception with fundamental innovations in vaulting technology. A further corollary of Giedion's historical analysis is the abolition of the single viewpoint perspective, which has promoted an increasingly dynamic conception of form. Both Utzon's Opera House and Gropius' Bauhaus were designed to be experienced from multiple viewpoints. Professor Giedion's analysis of the Bauhaus (fig. 11) could equally describe the Sydney Opera House '. . . it is necessary to go round it on all sides, to see it from above as well as below'.[50] Utzon substituted the sphere for the cube, and in so doing created a freer voluptuous mingling of form (fig. 12).

Ancient architectural complexes almost invariably followed a rigid hierarchical disposition of symbols which were based on the current conception of cosmic order. Such rigid ideal systems of order are largely irrelevant today. A new organic conception of order is unfolding, which permits spontaneous random modifications to the architecture without detracting from its wholeness. Two different approaches may be discerned.

1. The megastructure consists of a three-dimensional structure and services grid into which functional spaces may be inserted as required. The addition or subtraction of architectural tissue from the supporting structure does not detract from its visual wholeness. The Japanese Metabolists and John Andrews frequently use megastructures in their designs.

2. The concept of group form developed from the study of primitive vernacular architecture. Whole structures are made by the repetition of standard units. The advantage of this system is that it permits units to be added or subtracted at random without adversely affecting the architectural composition. Group form is really spontaneous composition.

The standardization of elements also facilitates the industrialization of building.

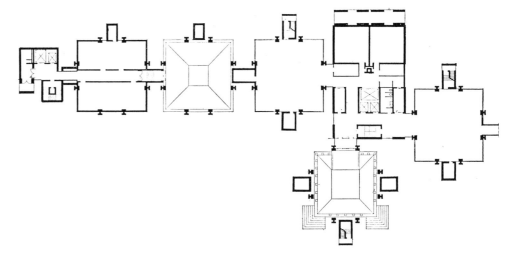

8, 9. The exploitation of building services as a source of architectural expression tends to subordinate real functions to aesthetic concerns. Richards Research Building, University of Pennsylvania, Philadelphia. Architect: Louis Kahn, 1961–4.
8. Ground floor plan.
9. View of towers facing the garden.

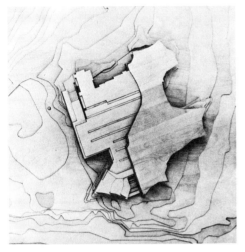

10. A surf of pines breaks upon the concave bays of Reima Pietilä's Students' Union at Otaniemi, Finland, 1964–6, so that the distinction between architecture and landscape is dissolved.

11. The potential enrichment of architecture experienced from a multiplicity of viewpoints was exploited in the massing of the Bauhaus at Dessau. Architect: Walter Gropius, 1926.

Jørn Utzon's architecture is an inspired development of group form (fig. 13). His public housing at Elsinore and Fredensborg are obvious applications of the principle. Less obvious is the Sydney Opera House. The geometry of the shells was derived from two parent spheres and so, in a very real sense, it too fulfills the definition of group form. Utzon calls this additive architecture.

Moshe Safdie applied group form to the problems of high-density housing. The repetitive nature of the basic form allows Safdie to standardize the building elements, thus facilitating factory production. A strict Neumannic geometry governs his architecture.

In Shinto architecture, the column and beam were assimilated into the symbolic milieu, where they served dual spiritual and structural roles. The rich imagery of the column and beam permeates the futurist schemes of the Metabolists (fig. 14). Their architecture is a type of trabeated sculpture which establishes an inner affinity with primitive Japanese consciousness.

James Stirling's architecture is a kind of industrial sculpture (fig. 15). His vocabulary is drawn from the English functional tradition of industrial building. Stirling exploits the industrial vernacular to create a virile poetry of transparency.

Frei Otto is exclusively concerned with an architecture of tension (fig. 16). He has dispensed with traditional aesthetic values in the search for structural economy. The supreme grace of many of Frei Otto's structures belies their complexity. He seems to prove that tension is beautiful.

It is questionable whether the third generation has incorporated the horizontal plane as a constituent element of its architecture, as claimed by Giedion. They have employed the horizontal plane in two clearly defined contexts, however, and this occasional practice hardly warrants its inclusion as a general trend. Horizontal platforms or stylobates occur in Mayan, Aztec, Greek, Egyptian and Indian architecture. They were an invaluable compositional device for binding the individual buildings together. As an extension of the architecture, they assisted in relating the architectural and landscape forms. Utzon alone among the third generation has pursued this aspect of the horizontal plane. Aalto and Wright used it on various occasions.

Artificial platforms are frequently used to separate pedestrian and vehicular traffic. The increasing complexity of urban land use and circulation patterns has encouraged the vertical separation of conflicting functions. The third generation architects have extended its application and widened its definition to include artificial building platforms.

The Renaissance revival of classical architecture by an educated elite began the estrangement of architecture from the popular consciousness. Classical European architecture became the prerogative of the ruling classes. Bernard Rudofsky describes it as: 'An anthology of buildings of, by, and for the privileged'.[51] Early modern architecture, unintentionally, confirmed the separation of the architect and community. The urge to re-establish contact with the aboriginal roots and reconvene a cul-

12. The roof vaults of the Sydney Opera House achieve a comparable though freer mingling of forms to that noted by Sigfried Giedion in the Bauhaus. Architect: Jørn Utzon, 1957–67.

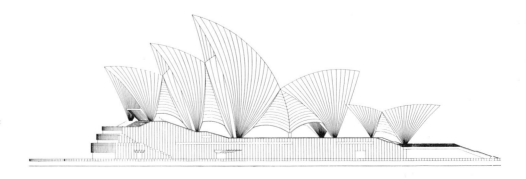

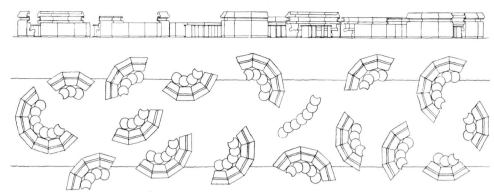

13. The variety of permutations obtained from a system of components enabled Jørn Utzon to develop patterns of public seating to promote social contact.

14. The contrived levitation of a beam-building revives the ancient Japanese symbolism of beam and column which permeates the monumental imagery of the Metabolists. Columbarium. Architect: Kiyonori Kikutake, 1966.

15. The unselfconscious nineteenth-century tradition of iron and glass evoked a virile poetry of transparency which animates the History Faculty Building at Cambridge University. Architect: James Stirling, 1964–7.

16. The striving towards increasing lightness motivated Frei Otto's pursuit of more efficient structural forms. Swiss National Exhibition at Lausanne, 'Snow and Rocks' Pavilions. Structural consultant: Frei Otto, 1964.

tural communism had a significant impact on postwar literature, music and art. In architecture, it led to empathy with unselfconscious architecture and identification with popular contemporary culture.

The third generation architects have bartered individual expression for expression of community. Unselfconscious architecture provides a model of an anonymous architecture organized for and expressing collective values. Today architecture seeks to express the collective consciousness.

Forty years separate Le Corbusier's sketches of Mediterranean vernacular architecture and his design at Ronchamp. Early modern architects passed over vernacular architecture as a source of expression because it did not coincide with their vision of a machine architecture, but there is ample evidence none the less that they were aware of the buildings of primitive mankind. Rudolph Schindler sketched Pueblo Indian villages in 1915. In the thirties, Le Corbusier flew over the oasis hutments of Mz'ab desert tribesmen, which inspired his comment that they were 'men in tune with fundamentals'.[52] The fundamentals alluded to were probably the tribesmen's preference for primary forms, a prejudice Corbusier shared. Bruno Taut published his pioneer study of the traditional Japanese house in 1937, *Houses and Peoples of Japan*.

However, a true interest in regionalism did not appear until the fifties. It gathered momentum throughout this period, culminating in 1965 with Bernard Rudofsky's photographic exhibition, *Architecture Without Architects*. Under the influence of the machine aesthetic, architects disguised traditional materials as machine products. The example of Le Corbusier at the Unité d'Habitation and the Maisons Jaoul strengthened the Brutalists' attack on this misuse of materials. In 1954 the Smithsons proclaimed:

'What is new about the New Brutalism among movements is that it finds its closest affinities not in past architectural styles, but in peasant dwelling forms. It has nothing to do with craft. We see architecture as a direct result of a way of life.'[53]

Such ideas were by no means restricted to the Smithson-Aldo van Eyck axis. Jørn Utzon visited Morocco in 1948. His housing at Elsinore and Fredensborg re-enacts the sculptural unity of landscape and building which he found in the Moroccan hill towns. Three projects—Aalto's Town Hall at Säynätsalo (1956), Atelier 5's Siedlung Halen (1961) and Paul Rudolph's Yale University Married Students' Housing (1962, fig. 17)—begin with the primitive archetype of the Italian hill-town. Aalto closed his attack on the Miesian cube with the purposeful use of natural materials and uninhibited disposition of forms which enjoin the primitive darkness of the enclosing woods.

The genius of a people asserting itself in folk culture has long been recognized as a rich source of artistic invention. The Grimm Brothers pioneered the methodical collection of folk tales. Their awareness of popular culture anticipated by over a centu-

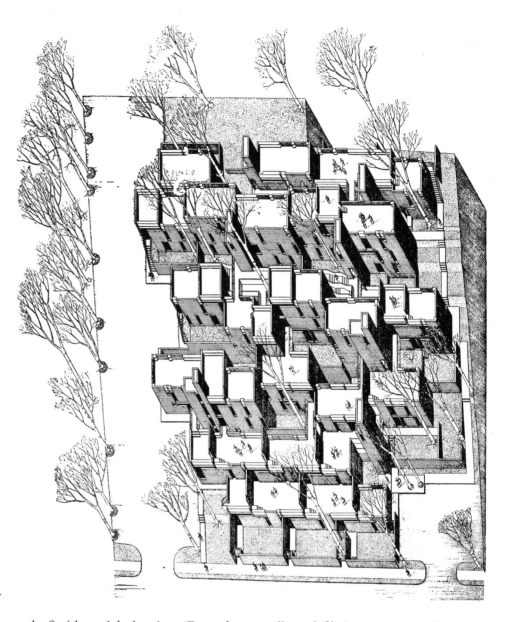

17. The primitive archetype of the Italian hill town re-appeared in the Yale University Married Students' Housing. Architect: Paul Rudolph, 1962.

ry the Smithsons' declaration: 'But today we collect ads'[54]. Consciousness of contemporary popular culture has been slow in developing, inhibited partly by the prestige of classical forms. The divergence of the machine aesthetic from the reality of mass production for mass culture created a barrier of taste between architects and the popular environment.

When Marshall McLuhan arrived at Cambridge in the late thirties, he found that Wyndham Lewis had already started studies on pop culture. He admits that in writing *The Mechanical Bride: Folklore of Industrial Man* (1951), he was merely trailing behind some interesting predecessors. Unlike McLuhan, who had the example of Lewis and James Joyce, modern architects were in possession of an aesthetic code which, as it turned out, could not have been more different from the aesthetic of consumer goods in the fifties.

The object of consumer product design was to promote sales, because a large market was essential to the success of mass production. Rational design principles were subordinated to the need to invest products with emotive qualities beyond pure function which could appeal to potential purchasers. The commercial product designers evolved an aesthetic based on popular images of power, sex and other forms of

18. The Pop functionalism of 1955 Bertone coachwork undermined the Bauhaus aesthetic equation.

19, 20. Robert Venturi championed the vitality of main street (19) against Peter Blake's comparison with the aridity of the University of Virginia (20).

social emulation. Galled by industries' failure to conform to modern architecture's patent machine aesthetic, leading architectural critics fired a prolonged burst of self-indulgent invective at commercial culture. An outraged *Architectural Review* (June 1955) led the assault on urban mess or 'subtopia'. Peter Blake clubbed 'pop' in the United States with *God's Own Junkyard*.

The English Independent Group consisting of Paolozzi, the Smithsons, Henderson, Banham and McHale uncovered an alternative response to the environment which Warhol summarized as 'Pop art is liking things'[55]. A new casual attitude towards popular culture emerged from the group meetings of 1954–5, based on a common pleasure in movies, advertisements, science fiction, automobiles and pop music. Their mass-produced urban culture was predominantly American, originating in Hollywood, Detroit and Madison Avenue.

A number of significant attitudes emerged from the forays of the Independent Group and the later succession of Archigram to pop leadership (1957–61). The machine aesthetic and pure functionalism were found wanting (fig. 18). A *rapprochement* between the architect and the environment 'as found' became possible. Charles Jencks points out with restrained glee that the 'pop theorists merely took the photos in the 1950 *Architectural Review* devoted to "the mess that is man-made America" and changed the captions'.[56]

In America, Robert Venturi exploded Peter Blake's comparison of the chaos of commercial main street with the orderliness of the University of Virginia with 'Is not main street almost all right . . . but the pictures in this book *(God's Own Junkyard)* that are supposed to be bad are often good'.[57] (figs. 19, 20)

Cedric Price and the Archigram Group orbited an entire vocabulary of concepts into the architectural consciousness in the late fifties. Archigram depth-charged establishment modern with a clarion imagery of expendability, mobility, change, light-weight-pneumatic, plug-in and instant city. They poached images from every conceivable source, including consumer technology, and cooked them into appetizing urban forms. The orientation was futurist and anti-architecture within the definition of architecture as monumental.

Strangely enough, it is in the lightweight structures and collapsible shelters devised by a straight technologist, Frei Otto, that the hot imagery of Archigram finds its most complete expression. His roofs for the 1972 Munich Olympic stadia are instant-city realized. The Metabolists' emphasis on change and servicing provides a superficial link with Archigram. On closer inspection, however, their obsession with a monumental public symbolic milieu anchors them in the historical continuum and excludes them from the futurist anticipations of Archigram. The *avant-garde's* devotion to its plastic blow-ups and 'pneu-world' and predictable denunciation of the heavyweight monumental world of the establishment sacrificed the real complexity and ambiguity inherent in such a confrontation.

The post-war era witnessed a major breakdown in architectural belief. The driving force behind anti-architecture was the desire to dispense with aesthetics (fig. 21). Anti-architecture put process before product, minimizing traditional architectural concerns. It was symptomatic of a deepfelt frustration with the medium of architecture which prevented architects from attacking problems directly. Modern architecture promulgated a single architectural language for the environment. Not surprisingly, it turned out to be insufficiently flexible to encompass the variety and complexity of modern life. McLuhan identifies the source of the difficulty in the following terms '. . . our personal experience sets up one grid between us and reality. Our culture adds one. Our language and our media system tighten the mesh'.[58]

The juxtaposition of aesthetic systems between the architect and reality complicates the statement and solution of problems. Anti-architecture is born of the faith that it is possible to sweep aside the personal, cultural and linguistic grids and so attain a functionalist Valhalla. Reyner Banham concludes *Theory and Design in the First Machine Age* with the exhortation that 'the architect who proposes to run with technology knows now that he is in fast company and that, in order to keep up, he may have to emulate the Futurists and discard his whole cultural load, including the professional garments by which he is recognized as an architect'.[59]

Banham's great achievement has been to show that try as they might, the first generation of modern architects were unable to dump their cultural load. Such an outcome is surprising considering the crucial role of pattern language as the medium of form production.

Architects use pattern languages and the pattern languages use them. Philosophers in the eighteenth century recognized the irrationality of language and invented a corrective methodology known as logic. Mathematics is simply a purer more exact language of reason. They did not attempt to dispense with language as the medium of rational discourse. The challenge facing the third generation is to evolve similar tools for aligning the pattern languages with reality. Christopher Alexander has already travelled a long way in this direction. The third generation no longer insists on a single inclusive pattern language for the environment, but recognizes that architecture can and should be both poetry and prose. They acknowledge the need for a number of languages to express the diversity of situations and the richness of life.

21. Reyner Banham's pneumatic standard of living package is the apotheosis of anti-architecture.

## Jørn Utzon

It is a measure of Jørn Utzon's creativity that he has escaped the gravitational pull of his Scandinavian heritage, taking ideas from outside (Mayan, Aztec and Japanese architecture) in pursuance of his own necessities. He was born in Denmark in 1918 and studied at the Royal Academy of Art in Copenhagen under Steen Eiler Rasmussen. The period of Utzon's life between 1945 and 1957 was one of absorption, assembling together a great variety of places and people and integrating these experiences into a comprehensive and coherent design philosophy. He worked for a time with Gunnar Asplund and Alvar Aalto (1945) and visited Wright at Taliesin. Henri Laurens strongly influenced his perception of sculptural form as suspended in space. He was especially attracted to primitive organic manifestations of architecture, and travelled extensively in Morocco, Mexico, China, Nepal, India and Japan. Utzon's involvement in competitions provided an opportunity to experiment with a variety of themes and integrate them into a mature philosophy. He built little. Then in 1957 he won the international competition for the Sydney Opera House which occupied the next decade of his professional life. The defeat of the incumbent New South Wales Labour Government in 1966 established forces of opportunism and revisionism subjecting the project to intense political stresses and interference. It sacrificed the subtle genius of Utzon's conception. The new Liberal Government's obstructionist tactics and determination to convert the Opera House into a Liberal Party monument forced Utzon to abandon the project. The government required a puppet administration which would implement its political revisions. Utzon summed up the entire affair succinctly with the phrase: 'malice in blunderland'. In 1967, he returned to Denmark where he has been busy on a wide variety of new schemes.

Sigfried Giedion announced Utzon's candidacy as Le Corbusier's successor to the leadership of the modern architectural movement in Europe by discreetly inserting a full chapter on his work in the fifth edition of *Space, Time and Architecture*. Giedion's intimacy and identification with the interests of the first generation leadership caused him to overvalue the artistic benefits of unity and continuity. Architecture is not politics. From the historian's point of view, Utzon possessed a number of tactical and artistic advantages over other contenders. He had not been active in the disbandment of C.I.A.M. and his architecture preserved a balance between the demands of reason and feeling which affirmed the continuity of modern architecture. These observations were subsidiary to Sigfried Giedion's estimate of Jørn Utzon as the most creative and original of the younger generation of architects in Europe.

Jørn Utzon's work prefigured the third generation's conversion to an organic conception of environmental order which displaced the first generation's rational bias. The inapplicability of the first generation's rigid rationalistic and extrinsic formulae as templates for structuring the environment forced architects among Utzon's generation to investigate relatively freer, intrinsic systems of order. Almost without exception—Roche and Stirling—the third generation acquired an organic outlook which involved taking instructions from the environment instead of enforcing preconceived rationalistic structures upon it. Wright's architecture is usually understood as a romantic nineteenth-century liaison with nature. At the heart of his understanding of the organic was the insistence that the designer listen to the environment. Utzon followed his understudy of Gunnar Asplund and Alvar Aalto (1945) with a visit to Taliesin West and Taliesin East where he spent a short time with Frank Lloyd Wright (1949). He thus learned to work with nature.

*Buildings and Projects*

Architect's own house, Hellebaek, North Zealand, 1952
House at Holte, near Copenhagen, 1953
Kingo Houses, near Elsinore, Zealand, 1956–60
Sydney Opera House, Australia, 1957–67
High School at Elsinore, Zealand, 1958 (First prize in competition)
Bank Melli, Teheran, Iran, 1959
Competition scheme for World Exhibition, Copenhagen, 1959
Elvira competition for town on Mediterranean Sea, 1960
Terrace houses at Fredensborg, North Zealand, 1962–3
Birkehøj housing estate, Elsinore, 1963
Zürich Theatre, 1964 (First prize in competition)
Art Gallery and Museum, Silkeborg, 1963
Farum Town Centre, 1966
Utsep Møbler flexible furniture components, 1968
Furniture for public buildings, 1968
Espansiva Byg A/S Timber Component House System, 1969
School centre with technical colleges, Herning, 1969
Jeddah Stadion, Saudi-Arabia, 1969

1, 2. Architect's own house at Hellebaek, North Zealand, 1952.
1. The house, seen from the drive.
2. Plan. Key: 1 study, 2 dining area, 3 kitchen zone, 4 fireplace, 5 living area, 6 entrance, 7 bedroom, 8 bathroom, 9 terrace, 10 garage, 11 heating plant, 12 pergola.

3, 4. House at Holte, near Copenhagen, 1953.
3. Western aspect overlooking lake.
4. This house was framed from a simple system of prefabricated posts and beams, a forerunner of later system generating systems.

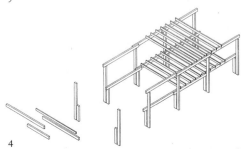

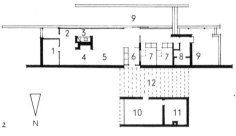

Unselfconscious architecture was the route taken by the European mind in reestablishing contact with the organic domain of environmental structure. A visit to Morocco in 1948 supplied Utzon with a model of molecular form generation or 'additive architecture'. The inspiration of unselfconscious architecture profoundly influenced him. The conjunction of Jørn Utzon and Christopher Alexander's concepts of environmental structure arises because both begin with the same model—unselfconscious architecture. Their contrasting modes of working (Utzon is intuitive and Alexander is rational) differentiate their conclusions. Utzon's architecture provides a superb demonstration of Alexander's theory of system-generating systems. The morphology of his architectural environments is defined by the combinatorial patterns of the generic forms or elements—Alexander's 'kit of parts'. The housing at Elsinore (1956) and Fredensborg (1962) were fairly simple expositions of the idea (pp. 46, 47).

Utzon reduced the major functional problems associated with the Sydney Opera House (1957–67, pp. 50–53)—the structural vaults and the cladding system, the glass wall and plywood mullion system, the plywood acoustic shells and the corridor panel system—into basic kits of parts suitable for prefabrication. *Zodiac 14* included a typically Alexanderian illustration of a system-generating system, a picture of telephone components accompanied by the caption 'put them together and dial anywhere'. Three recent projects, the Farum Town Centre (1966, p. 56), the Espansiva Timber Component House System (1969, pp. 48, 49), and the Utsep Møbler flexible furniture components (1968, p. 57) investigated at a public, domestic and personal scale the opportunities for flexible environmental structures based on a limited alphabet of components or space cells. Arup Associates adopted a similar approach for their design of heavily serviced laboratory buildings.

The decomposition of complex environmental structures into molecular components permits standardization for factory production. Utzon benefited from the Scandinavian tradition of collaborative design with industry which gave the machine a human face. The implementation of the concept of system-generating systems enabled Utzon to resolve the conflicting demands of standardization for repetitive production without sacrificing the flexibility essential for negotiating the indeterminate terrain of human functions.

Expression is simply a device for enhancing architectural meaning. The Renaissance championed the individual artistic genius. Utzon substituted the anonymous expression of collective consciousness and symbiosis with landscape in place of rampant individual expression. He reasserted the right of the anonymous expression over and beyond the purely utilitarian, in defiance of the first generation's functional puritanism. The housing projects at Elsinore and Fredensborg were purged of idiosyncratic expressionism. Their collective forms extend the lessons of unselfconscious architecture through a mono-material manipulation of brick vernacular details and simple cubic forms which attain an unbroken sculptural unity of architecture and landscape. The anonymous form-generating structural system of Gothic architecture illuminates Jørn Utzon's design intent in the Sydney Opera House: 'if you think of a Gothic church you are closer to what I have been aiming at . . . looking at a Gothic church, you never get tired, you will never be finished with it . . . this interplay (of light and movement) . . . makes it a living thing'.[60]

Sensitivity to inner relationships controls the marriage of Utzon's architecture to the landscape. The resonance of the architecture within the landscape is intensified by simplifying the architectural composition to two dominant visual elements, the horizontal roof and floor planes, which model the sky and earth as spatial co-ordinates. The physical tension induced by Utzon's opposition of hovering roofs and strong earth-hugging platforms defines the architectural space. He confided '. . . there is

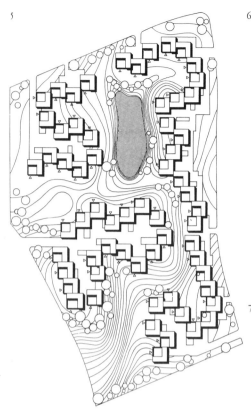

5–9. Kingo Houses, near Elsinore, Zealand, 1956–60.
5. The housing layout responds to the topography.
6. By adhering to the same *leitmotif* and the same building materials, the variegated shapes are impressively integrated.
7. Each house encloses a private garden court.
8. Sectional view.
9. Plan.

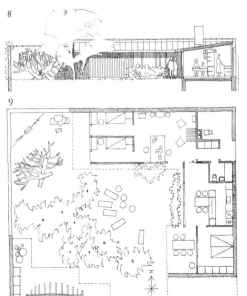

magic in the play between roof and platform'.[61] The edges of the platform and underside of the roofs mark the transition from architecture to landscape. The omission of vertical structure from Utzon's *esquisses* evokes a trance-like quality of ascension and cosmic awareness. This ideal of a nihilist architecture in which architectural space becomes indistinguishable from landscape space also appears in the writings of Banham and the schemes of Archigram. Kenzo Tange's Festival Plaza Roof for Expo '70 attempted to realize the dissolution of architecture contained in Utzon's sketches.

The horizontal platform assumes a multiple significance for Utzon as a constituent element of architectural expression. It binds his buildings to the earth and creates an artificial terrain; it elicits an emotional affinity with the early origins of architecture (Mayan and Aztec terrace building) and provides a simple means of separating vehicular and pedestrian traffic. Utzon's recognition of the sculptural richness of artificial platforms is tempered by the social insight that 'in a traditional Japanese house the floor attracts you as the wall does in a European House. You want to sit close to the wall in a European house, and here in Japan you want to sit on the floor and not walk on it'.[62] The Sydney Opera House and submissions for the Elsinore

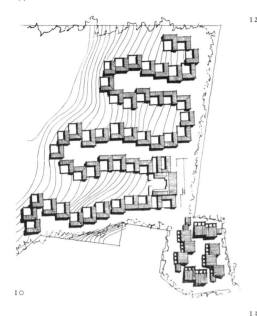

10

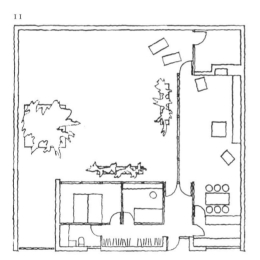

11

12

13

10–13. Terrace houses at Fredensborg, North Zealand, 1962–3.

10. Site plan.

11. House plan.

12. Adjustment of house units to sloping site provides sculptural interest.

13. The vernacular of brick and pantile imparts a unity akin to unselfconscious architecture.

High School (p. 54), Elvira Mediterranean community and Zürich Theatre competitions (p. 54) all incorporated a powerful platform or earth deck. The stepped horizontal planes of the Zürich Theatre roofscape (1964) redeployed the magnificent articulated folded concrete slabs with which Ove Arup bridged the car entrance (60 m) at Sydney. A fascination with primitive earth form pervades Utzon's shaping of his platforms. The auditoria at Sydney recall Inca theatres deftly carved out of the Andes mountainside and fitted to the contours of the surrounding terrain. The caves at Tatung, west of Peking, visited by Utzon in 1957, contain hundreds of Buddha statues and inspired the project for an Art Gallery and Museum in Silkeborg (1963, p. 55). The gallery chambers were sunk into the body of the earth in kiln-like pits lit from above. No platform was required because the architect returned his building to the earth.

The union of the organic and geometric in the architecture of Jørn Utzon and Moshe Safdie is an outstanding, though by no means universal attribute of the third generation. Professor Giedion observed that 'usually in architecture, the organic and the geometric are strictly separated, they run parallel to one another but they never meet . . . rational geometric forms were characteristic of the early period of modern

14. Birkehøj, Elsinore. Site plan of housing estate, 1963.

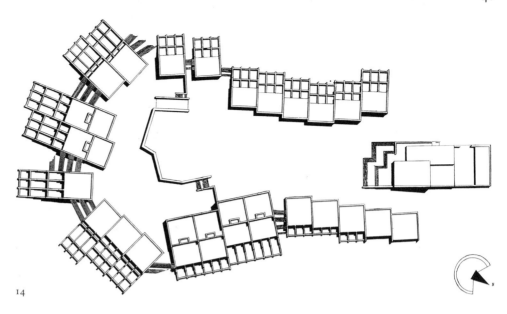

14

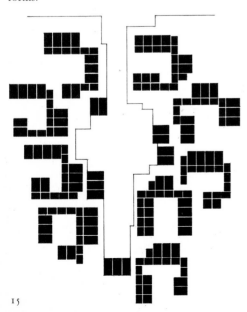

15

15–18. Espansiva Byg A/S Timber Component House System, one-family houses, 1969.
15. Individual variety integrated within the group form by means of a recurring kinship of the forms.

architecture'.[63] He then goes on to assert the synthesis of the rational-geometric and the mystic-organic principles in third generation architecture. It is probable that what has occurred is a mutual exchange. The third generation maintains two principles; the organic-geometric and the rational-mystic (Archigram, James Stirling). Two spheres, one for each auditorium, served as a genetic code which generated the external form of the concrete vaults for the Sydney Opera House. This spatial geometry ensured that the segments obtained by slicing into the two standard spheres could be easily defined mathematically, thus facilitating the repetitive prefabrication of the component structural elements. These spheres are equivalent to Christopher Alexander's 'seeds of the environment' and the common parentage of the vaults imprints a 'wholeness' on the external environment. The interior structural plywood acoustic shells were similarly derived from two standard cylinders. Utzon likened the dynamics of their form generation to the cyclical motion of waves.

The contradictory interplay between inside and outside spatial needs was expressed by the separate statement of the exterior vaults and interior acoustic shells. Hardline functionalists criticized Utzon for failing to express the inside on the outside. Setting aside the historical naïveté of this argument, the writings of Robert Venturi provide independent support for Utzon's decision that *'contrast between the inside and the outside can be a major manifestation of contradiction*. However, one of the powerful twentieth-century orthodoxies has been the necessity for continuity between them: the inside should be expressed on the outside'.[64] (author's italics) The contrapuntal interplay of forms enclosed within forms initiated at Sydney is matched at a domestic scale by Venturi's Frug House Scheme 1 (p. 156). The extreme sensitivity of Utzon's response to landscape and people and his sympathy for the anonymous client imbue his architecture with an enduring quality of human richness. His sketch layouts for the Kingo Houses near Elsinore come alive with domestic anticipations: a boat under construction in the courtyard, children caught in a swordfight. In a modest fashion, Utzon designed the housing as a non-assertive incomplete environment to be expanded and modified by the occupants. It is surely a human architecture full of possibilities. The placing of the houses willingly responds to slight changes in the slope of the land.

The Sydney Opera House concept concentrated the unconscious meanings of its ur-

16, 17. Plan configurations generated from the standard elements.
18. Stressed-skin façade elements, window and door units.

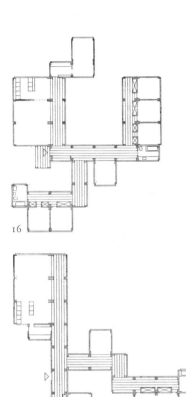

16

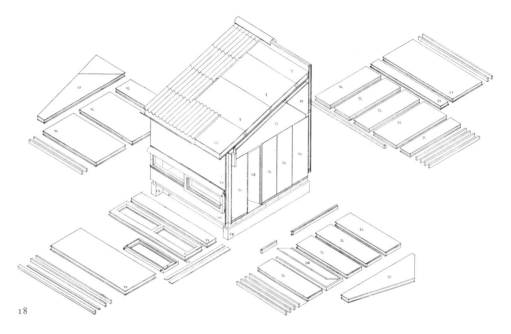

18

17

ban context in the same way as Notre Dame, situated on the Ile de Cité, does for Paris. It manifests the spirit of the city, and in so doing has become a popular symbol. Utzon tuned the Zürich theatre to the existing architectural environment, so that it too binds the scattered neighbourhood into a recognizable unit without betraying its own expression.

It would be misleading to equate Jørn Utzon too closely with the third generation; nevertheless, he stands as its most compelling and original visionary.

19, 20. Prototype house, erected at Gammel Hellebaek, North Zealand.
19. Street façade.
20. Garden court.

19

20

21

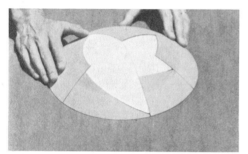

22, 23

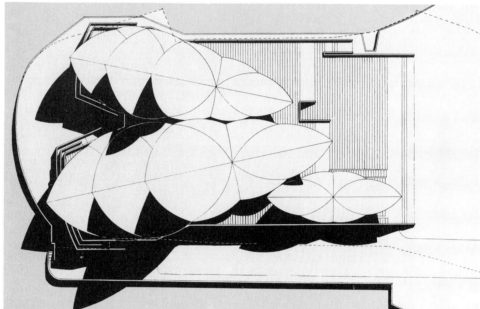

24

25

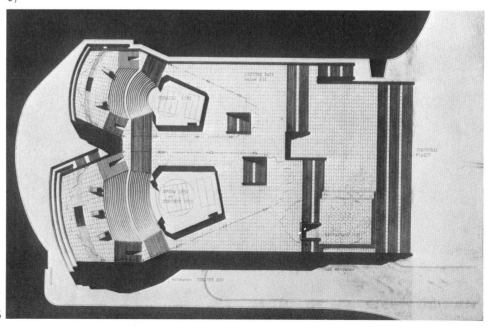

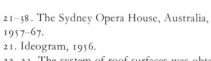

21–38. The Sydney Opera House, Australia,
1957–67.
21. Ideogram, 1956.
22, 23. The system of roof surfaces was obtained
from a parent sphere explained by the spherical
model.
24. Model.
25. The exposed location of the Sydney Opera
House, sited on a promontory extending into
Sydney harbour, called for a sculptural shape.
26. The plan of the platform deck reveals the
contoured pedestrian terrain from which the roof
vaults rise.

26

27, 28

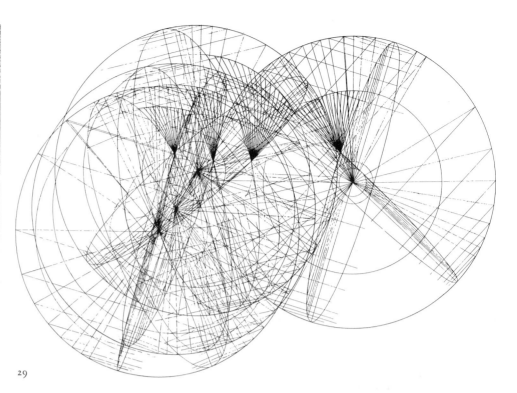

29

27, 28. The cyclical action of water particles in a
moving wave inspired Utzon's design of the
interior acoustic shells of the auditoria.
29. Geometrical development of the roof vaults
for the Major Hall in elevation.
30, 31. A cyclical wave motion generates the
section of each radial segment which composes
the acoustic shell.
32. Geometrical development of the superimposed profiles of the interior acoustic shells.

32

30, 31

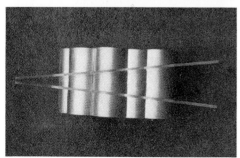

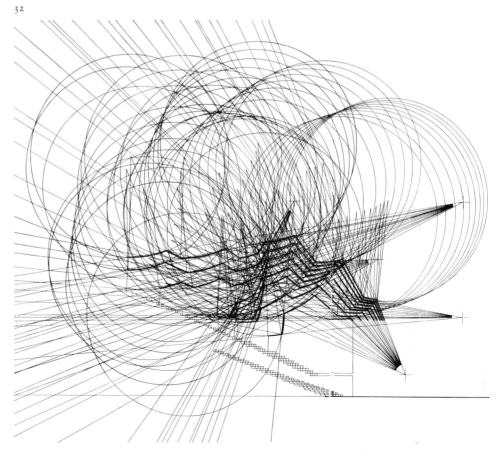

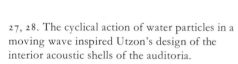

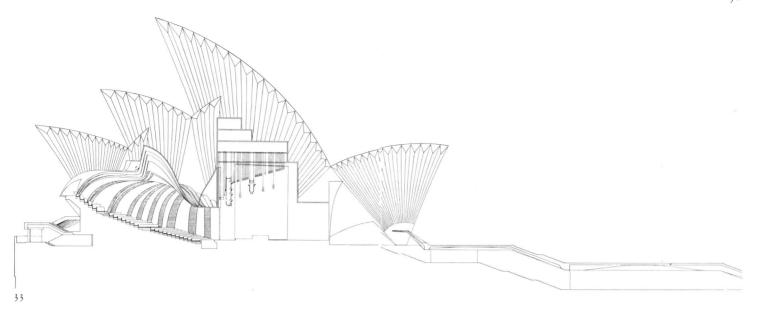

33

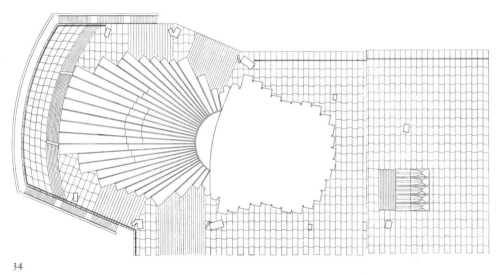

34

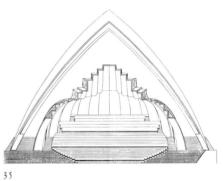

35

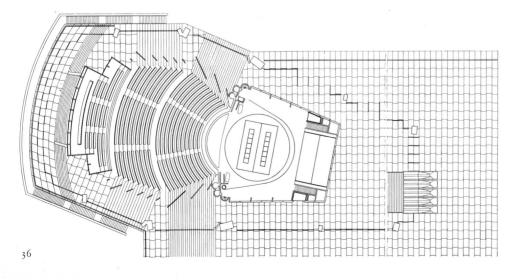

36

33. Longitudinal section through Minor Hall
showing elevation of auditorium and stage wall.
34. Roof plan of Minor Hall.
35. Cross section of Minor Hall.
36. Floor plan of Minor Hall.
37. Utzon's genius was to marry his building to
its marine environment in a perfect symbiosis of
architecture and landscape.
38. A cascade of white spherical vaults shelter the
performing halls.

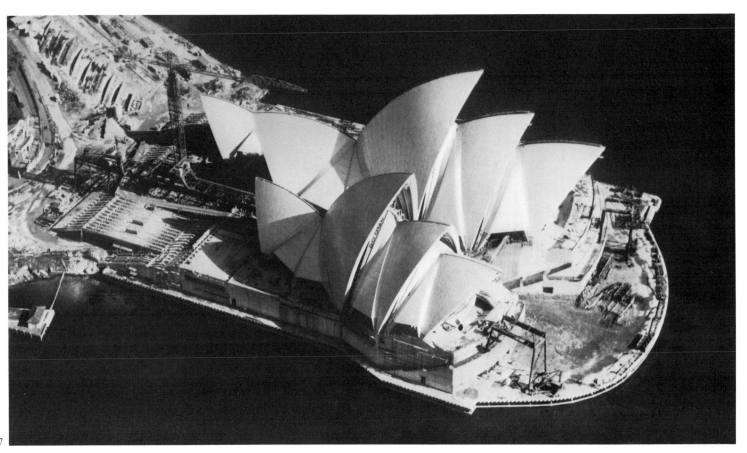

37

38

39–41. High School at Elsinore, Zealand. First prize in competition, 1958.
Section, roof plan, and ground floor platform.

42–44. Zürich Theatre. First prize in competition, 1964.
Longitudinal section, roof deck, and ground floor platform.

39

40

41

42

43

44

45–47. Competition scheme for World Exhibition, Copenhagen, 1959.
Section, roof deck, and ground floor platform.

48–51. Art Gallery and Museum in Silkeborg.
Project, 1963.
Longitudinal section, roof plan, ground floor plan, and gallery floor plan.

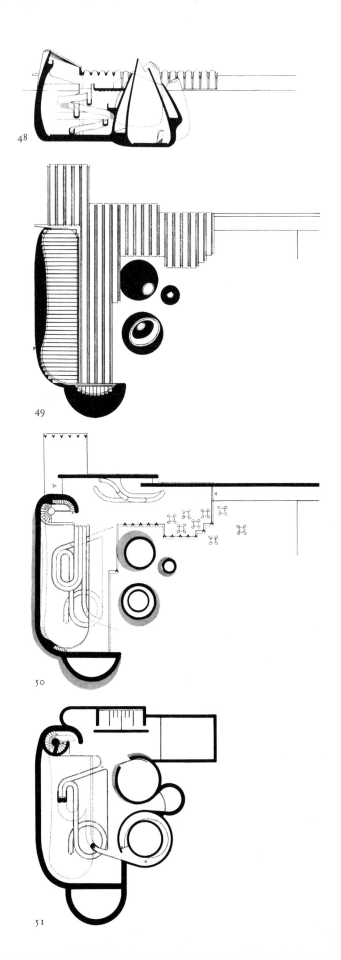

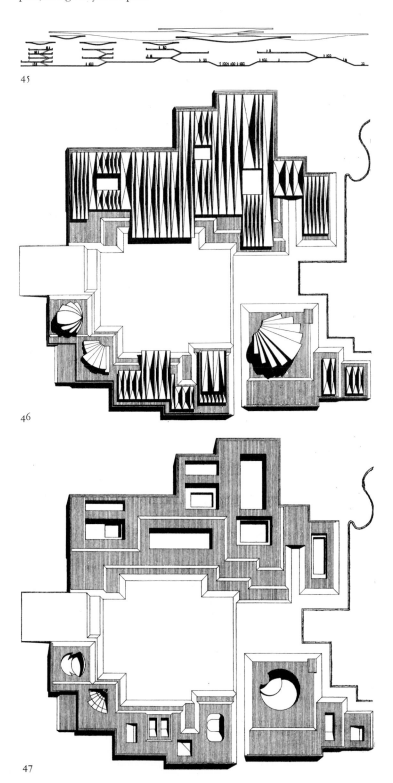

45

46

47

48

49

50

51

52

52, 53. School centre with technical colleges, Herning, 1969.
First stage model of school and plan.

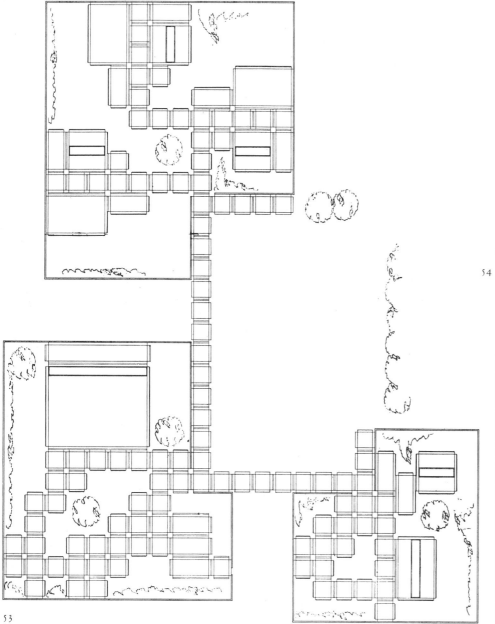

54. Farum Town Centre. Project, 1966. First stage model.

54

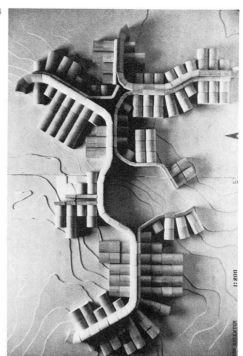

53

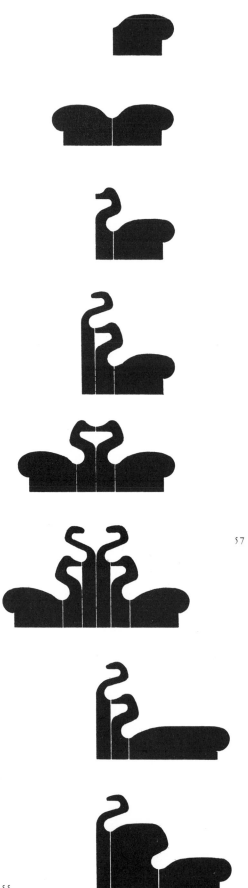

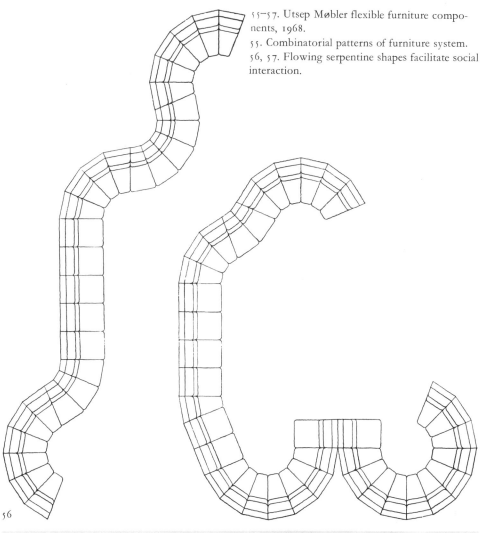

55–57. Utsep Møbler flexible furniture components, 1968.
55. Combinatorial patterns of furniture system.
56, 57. Flowing serpentine shapes facilitate social interaction.

56

57

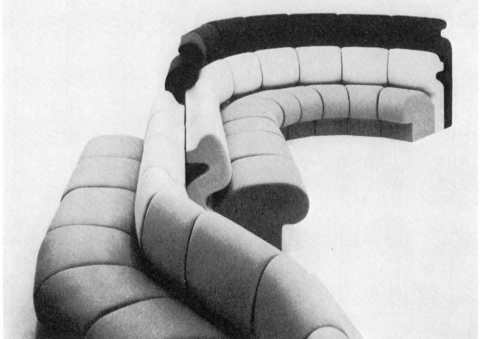

# Moshe Safdie

Moshe Safdie's environmental philosophy integrates a unique range of human encounters and rich vernacular landscapes. A sense of communal identity and fascination in organic life was fostered by his early life in Haifa, Israel. Safdie was born there in 1938 and emigrated to Canada with his parents at the age of fifteen. The insights obtained from a Central Mortgaging and Housing Corporation sponsored travelling fellowship (1959) looking at housing in North America—while Safdie was still a student at the McGill University School of Architecture—crystallized in his final thesis.

After graduation, Safdie worked with Sandy van Ginkel, who had been a close associate of Aldo van Eyck in Holland, interrupted by a year spent in Louis Kahn's office. Through van Ginkel, Safdie was involved in Expo '67—first on the master plan and then on Habitat. Safdie was twenty-six years old when he designed Habitat '67 (pp. 59–61) which implemented system 'C' as outlined in his undergraduate thesis (1961). Habitat survived numerous threats because of Safdie's extreme dedication and the sympathetic courageous support of men like Colonel Churchill. Five Habitat schemes followed the original—for Fort Lincoln, Nebraska, New York (pp. 62,63), Indian Carry (p. 62), Puerto Rico (pp. 64,65) and Jerusalem (p. 66) which elaborated the original theme with increasing geometrical sophistication. The exchange of ideas which resulted from his close friendship (begun in 1967) with Christopher Alexander confirmed and deepened his commitment to the creation of a contemporary vernacular in the tradition of spontaneous self-made environments.

The distinctive ideals of the third generation are most completely embodied in the architecture of Moshe Safdie. He harnessed the conceptual power of two separate streams of thought which flowed from the fifties, an interest in unselfconscious building as a model of democratic architecture, and the rediscovery of modern architecture's mission to industrialize building. Sandy van Ginkel put Safdie in touch with European thought and, in particular, the investigations by the Dutch *avant-garde* of spontaneously generated environments, the subject of Bernard Rudofsky's book *Architecture Without Architects*. The two streams of thought complemented one another. The principle of form generation exemplified by vernacular environments promised to resolve the conflicting demands of standardization, dictated by mass production, while providing a flexibility which responded to individual needs.

Moshe Safdie rejected the Renaissance tradition of fixed architectural compositions in favour of open vernacular building systems responsive to choice, change and growth. Kisho Noriaki Kurokawa's additive growth and Jørn Utzon's additive architecture resemble Safdie's expression of molecular forms in the Habitat series. In his undergraduate thesis, Safdie developed three building systems. The first consisted of structural frames rising thirty storeys high, with plug-in units located within the support structure by lift-slab technology; another consisted of panels and the third consisted of a system rising to twelve storeys and made up of load-bearing units. He proposed the plug-in concept three years before Peter Cook published it in *Archigram IV* in 1964. An early sketch by Le Corbusier (p. 59) suggested the simplistic separation of structure and enclosure functions, a first generation orthodoxy, and Kikutake revived it in his 1958 Mova-block proposal (p. 88). Safdie implemented the load-bearing system throughout the Habitat series—except in the case of New York Scheme II (p. 63)—because it avoided the structural redundancy of the plug-in concept.

Crystal morphology is determined by molecular structure and available chemical bonds. Similarly, the geometry of Safdie's standard space modules dictates the three-

1. Le Corbusier proposed the separation of structural and enclosure functions by inserting prefabricated dwelling *unités* in a structural frame.

2. One of the three-dimensional modular building systems considered for Habitat '67 by Moshe Safdie and later discarded for structural reasons renewed Le Corbusier's plug-in concept.

dimensional combinatorial patterns and hence the architectural morphology. They are a kind of genetic code for the environment. There is an affinity between Christopher Alexander's pattern languages and Safdie's structures. Whereas Alexander asserts that 'the seeds of the environment are pattern languages',[65] Safdie says '. . . we must try to find the genetic code of a particular environment. The genetic code produces an infinite number of adaptations, each in itself not finite—not buildings with beginnings and ends, but continuums capable of growth and change . . . In each case I search for a solution that is organically valid for that particular problem'.[66] Habitat '67 is a twentieth-century version of Mesa Verde, whose adobe clusters fan upward to touch the underside of a huge jutting slab of rock which shelters the large communal space in its protective shadow. Similarly, Habitat's helical cascade of corbelled load-bearing house modules—propped against the pedestrian-mechanical street and circulation towers—straddle the continuous public space.

The experience of Kibbutz life in Israel and the dense terraces of Haifa opened Safdie to the suggestions for urban morphology contained in primitive vernacular landscapes. Assembled from a vocabulary of repetitive components, the Aegean hill villages, the Arab hill towns and the Indian pueblos appeared to Safdie as true prototypes of industrialized building systems. By abandoning the act of creation and seeking instead the means of creating, he identified with the idea of vernacular which is made by men for themselves. The ideal of a building system which permits people to shape and modify their personal environment is a persistent theme running through third generation thought. Although circumstances and the technical complexity of Habitat '67 precluded user involvement, Safdie countered this by extending consumer choice through a wide variety of house plans. Subsequent projects, notably the San Francisco State College Union (p. 67) and the Arab Refugee Habitat (p. 66), amply testify to the sincerity of Safdie's intention to involve the building occupants in the design and construction phases of the building process.

Habitat '67 was dedicated to the exploration of new forms of housing which recreate in a high density environment the relationships and the amenities of the house and village. Fundamental to Safdie's patient search for new systems of form which promote environmental quality is the belief that 'having an outdoor space by your house, and daylight and the ability to identify your dwelling, are essential to survival'.[67]

The uncompromising functionalism of Safdie, reminiscent of Hannes Meyer, is conditioned by a thorough-going acceptance of the imperatives of industrialization and new technologies. At the core of his philosophy of architecture is the realization that it is essential to rethink building in terms of space cells instead of conventional panel systems if the twenty-five percent threshold of industrialization is to be breached. The industrialization of building assumes an urgency comparable to the industrialization of agriculture at an earlier age—shelter means survival. Safdie contends that industrialization requires a reorganization of relationships and an end to the architect's magnificent isolation from the building process.

Safdie's achievement in carrying through the Habitat experiment can be gauged by the fact that it focused the equivalent of two-and-a-half years research effort by the British Building Research Station on a single major problem. Louis Kahn's structural consultant, Dr. A. E. Komendant, testified that 'Habitat could have been built in its own right within reasonable time and economical limits if there had been a single executive authority completely in charge of all phases of the project'.[68] The commencement of work on the Puerto Rico Habitat (pp. 64, 65) in April 1970 at a cost of $17 per square foot confirmed August Komendant's assessment.

Sometimes the Fascist state is a more reliable indicator of architectural quality than the most experienced critic. In the thirties, the Nazis terrorized modern architects.

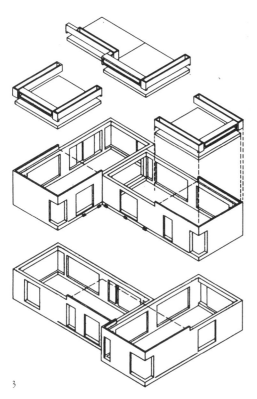

3

Three decades later, a resurgence of Fascism smashed Jørn Utzon's concept for the Sydney Opera House (1957–67) and suppressed Moshe Safdie's Students Union at the San Francisco State College (1968–9). Observing the role of the campus green as a focus of informal social activity, Safdie heaped up the Union building in a man-made hill which extended the grass and plant life over its inclined walls and terraces. Arched over the campus circulation cross-roads, the open hollowed-out hill invited students to wander over it and through it. The diversified spatial requirements necessitated a departure from the usual Habitat approach. For this reason, Safdie devised a 'Space Maker', based on a three-dimensional grid combining ninety-degree and forty-five degree axes in all three planes. Combinations of the standard bent pre-cast unit enabled him to generate an intricate variety of spatial scales and confirmed the environment's wholeness.

The San Francisco State College Union project is remarkable both as a design and as an experiment in student involvement. The board of trustees expressed its violent contempt for the democratic process by denying student access to Union funds for the purpose of construction. Moshe Safdie's sensitivity to student feelings and needs identified the building with student aspirations which effectively condemned the proposal in the repressive political atmosphere of State College.

The enormous ability of Moshe Safdie as an architect, and his commitment to the creation of humanly meaningful environments suggests that his future performance will further extend third-generation concepts into a new world.

3–8. Habitat '67, first phase, Montreal, 1964–7.
3. Basic relationship of boxes with roof slabs, planters.
4. Typical section through structure showing modular houses with garden terraces and elevated pedestrian streets.
5. A common morphology links Habitat '67 with vernacular hill villages.
6. The fractured crystals of Habitat's molecular forms recognize individual variability while preserving the unity of community concourse.
7. View of elevated pedestrian street.
8. Looking down from the roof terraces.

4

5

6

7

8

9

12

9–11. Indian Carry Habitat. Project, 1966.
9. View of model.
10. Typical cluster, plan of floor level.
11. Typical detail section.

10

13

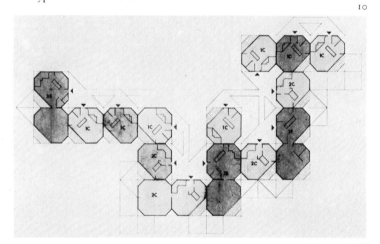

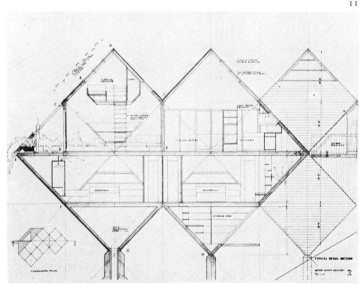

11

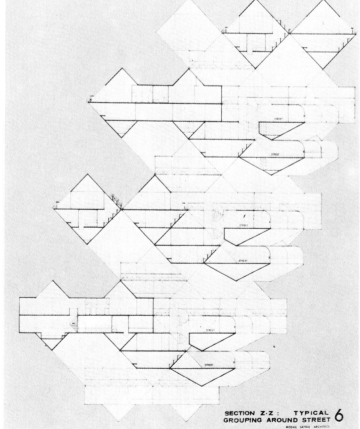

SECTION Z-Z : TYPICAL GROUPING AROUND STREET 6
MOSHE SAFDIE ARCHITECT

12, 13. New York Habitat, Scheme I. Project, 1968.
12. View of model.
13. Section of a typical grouping around street.

14–16. New York Habitat, Scheme II. Project, 1968.
14. Aerial view of model.
15. Plan, three-bedroom apartment.
16. Section showing the service with the catenary cables from which the housing units are suspended.

14

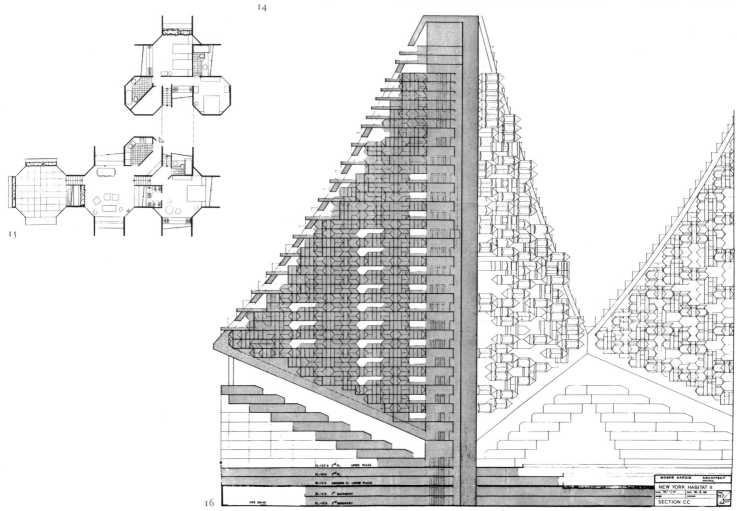

15

16

17

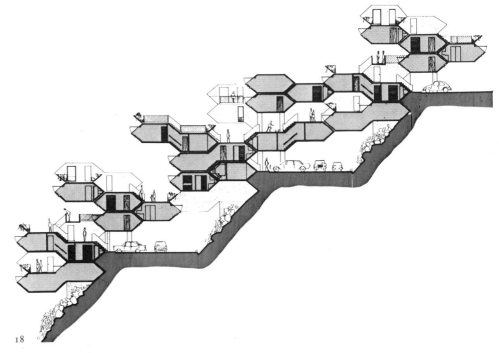

17–20. Puerto Rico Habitat. Project, 1968–71.

17. Octahedron housing units grow out of the hillside.

18. A section through the mountain showing the clusters spanning the service drives. The split level house module permits both internal and external circulation.

19. Model view of street.

20. Model view of housing cluster.

18

19

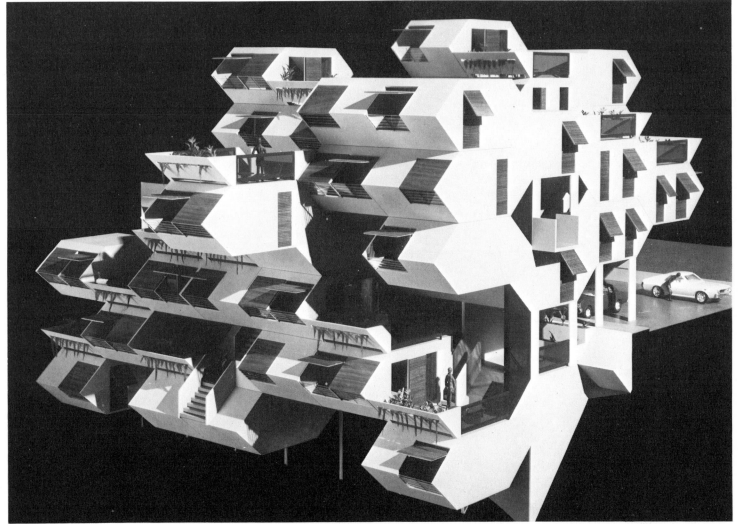

21

22

21, 22. Israel Habitat (Arab Refugee Self Help City), Manchat Hillside, Jerusalem. Project, 1969.
21. Overall view of the Jerusalem hillside showing the spiral roads spanned by housing clusters.
22. A typical housing cluster.

23–25. San Francisco State College Union. Project, 1968–9.
23. The man-made hill of the Student Union featured walk-up and planted walls.
24. Plan, third floor.
25. The basic system showing a repetitive element which generated large, medium and small rooms for different functions.

23

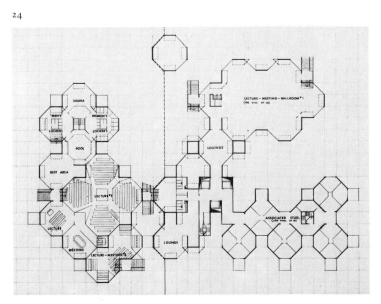

24

25

## Kisho Noriaki Kurokawa

Kisho Noriaki Kurokawa was one of the original founders of the Metabolism group. He is an intensely theoretical architect whose buildings somehow manage to survive a dreadful battering of prose to emerge with strong challenging forms. He was born in 1934 in Nagoya, studied architecture at Kyoto University (1957) and later took his master's degree at the University of Tokyo. For some time he was a member of the Kenzo Tange team, and collaborated on Tange's master plan for Tokyo. He opened his own studio in 1961. A lack of commissions for some years enforced an interest in theoretical writing and paper architecture. He contributed three building exhibits to Expo '70 at Osaka.

Architecture derived from the machine analogy possesses a fixity and mechanical perfection which preclude a freer more responsive relationship to the changing patterns of life. Recognition of the inadequacy of the machine idea led to the formulation of metabolism which attempted to substitute an analogy of architecture with biological processes in place of the orthodox analogy with machinery. The biological analogy was anticipated in the planning theory of Patrick Geddes. A number of third generation talents outside the metabolism circle, and including Utzon, Safdie and Habraken, refer to it. Kisho Noriaki Kurokawa's expositions of metabolism are often chaotic and confusing. The reader would be well advised to follow Noboru Kawazoe's advice 'not to be taken in by the words, *but should feel the theory behind them*'.[69] (author's italics)

The theory behind the words is surprisingly beautiful. Metabolism is the life system of organisms. Kurokawa includes change and growth within the meaning of metabolism. He distinguishes two types of organic change; material and energy metabolism. Material metabolism is concerned with the change and exchange of substances within a living organism. Energy metabolism is a theoretical expression of that process. Material metabolism suggests that the component elements of cities and buildings be classified according a hierarchy of metabolic cycles which relate the progressive rates of change and functional obsolescence. Master spacing is the planning device invented by Kurokawa for establishing the subjective hierarchy of spaces in relation to human beings, service life of components, and society. Technically, this produces a four step methodology:
1. Divide the spaces into basic units.
2. Divide the units into equipment units and living units.
3. Clarify the differences in metabolic rhythms among the unit spaces.
4. Clarify the connectors and joints among spaces with differing metabolic rhythms.
The hierarchy of master and servant spaces developed by Louis Kahn in his University of Pennsylvania research centre pioneered the principle.
Energy metabolism implies that people, things, and energy be considered as information. The dynamic patterns of information—so defined—within a city is its infrastructure. According to Kurokawa, the infrastructure in any context can be defined by the following method:
1. We conceive of people, things, and energy as information and attempt to clarify their flow patterns.
2. We combine these flow patterns in flexible ways.
3. We give order to the relationships between the information patterns and spatial units.
Le Corbusier anticipated Kurokawa's energy metabolism in his design of the Carpenter Center at Harvard. The Nishijin plan (p. 74) and the Children's Land Central Lodge (p. 75) are applications of the method.

*Buildings and Projects*

Agricultural cluster, Ise Region, 1960
Up-Ended Neighbourhood, 1960
Wall cluster, 1960
Town plan for Tokyo, 'Helicoidal' Towers, 1961
Precast concrete housing project, 1962
Labour Centre, Nishijin, 1962
Nitto Foods Plant, Sagae, Yamagata District, 1963
Honjima Hotel, 1964
National Children's Land: Andersen Memorial Hall, shelter and central lodge, 1964–5
Yamagata Hawaii Dreamland, 1967
Toshiba I.H.I. Pavilion, Expo '70, Osaka, 1968–70
Takara Beautilion, Expo '70, Osaka, 1968–70
Expo '70 housing capsule, attached to the Festival Plaza roof space frame, Osaka, 1968–70
Moving core MC-18, 1970
Business capsule BC-25, Ginza, Tokyo, 1970

1. Agricultural cluster, Ise Region, 1960.
A raised artificial earth platform supports mushroom living units.

2–4. Wall cluster, 1960.
2. Sketch. Living and work space is mounted on either side of an installation wall which rises from a horizontal structure which serves as an urban connector.
3. Plan.
4. Section. Static and mobile dwelling elements hang from brackets cantilevered from the inside face of the installation wall.

1

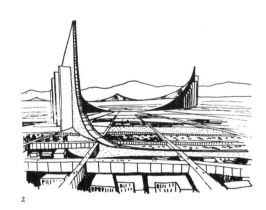

2

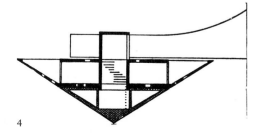

3

4

Organic growth, or metamorphosis, can be of two types: additive growth in such parts as bones and shell coverings, and multiplicative growth in the prototypical substance. External additive changes, such as occur in plants, characterize additive growth. Building expansion conforms to this definition. Additive growth is associated with simple tree-like hierarchical structures. The Nitto Foods Plant (p. 71) and the Toshiba I.H.I. Pavilion (p. 71) explore the possibilities of two and three dimensional additive growth. Utzon's 'additive architecture' and Arup Associates' system of laboratory design are applications of the principle.

Internal, active changes within cities such as the replacement of obsolete urban structures is analogous to multiplicative growth. Christopher Alexander has shown that cities consist of complex overlapping lattice structures, and the dual categories which persist throughout Kurokawa's theory of metabolism culminate in the distinction between 'porous spaces' and 'fibre form'.

Accordingly, 'porous spaces' are animal-like forms, involving cellular clusters of heterogeneous spaces. He employed porous spaces in his Helix City scheme of 1961 (p. 70) and the Yamagata Hawaii Dreamland (p. 77). Fibre form is a restatement by Kurokawa of traditional linear or finger planning. He describes it as homogeneous, plant-like forms extending in linear trunk and branch hierarchies.

The articulation of urban structure into permanent public support structures and private detachable units is a persistent theme running through Kurokawa's Utopian proposals. In the agricultural cluster scheme (p. 69), the support structure consisted of a horizontal reinforced concrete platform raised above the ground as a precaution against flooding.

The up-ended neighbourhood and Helix city proposals provide an intermediate transition from the horizontal support platform of the agricultural cluster to the vertical supports in the vertical wall city (p. 69). Kurokawa shares with Archigram a fascination for private, mass-produced housing capsules. The Expo '70 housing capsule (pp. 72, 73), suspended below Tange's Festival Plaza roof, is a prototype of the housing capsule envisaged in these earlier proposals. The business capsule residential tower to be built in the Tokyo Ginza district provides a practical demonstration of the idea (p. 73).

The broad scope of Kurokawa's talent, ranging from the unrestrained futurism of his metabolism schemes, through a sensitive evocation of tradition in the two pavilions in the National Children's Land at Yokohama, to the disciplined eclecticism of the Yamagata Hawaii Dreamland, confirms a consummate mastery of architectural form. Kisho Noriaki Kurokawa's critical awareness of the necessity to re-orientate modern architecture towards life by the assimilation of relevant biological processes provides a significant departure for future investigations.

5

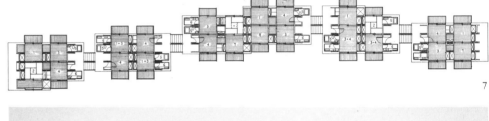

7

6

8

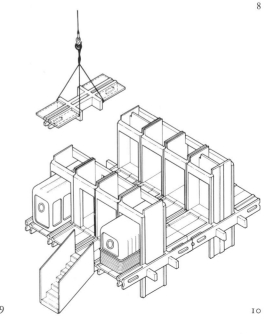

5, 6. Town plan for Tokyo. 'Helicoidal' towers. Model and sketch, 1961.

7–10. Precast concrete housing project, 1962.
7. Plan of linear apartment cluster.
8. Frontal view of model.
9. End view of model showing support structure and detachable dwelling modules.
10. Assembly sequence of prefabricated elements.

9

10

11

12

14

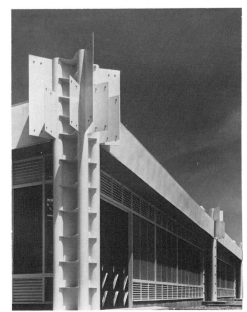

13

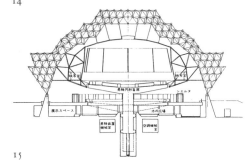

15

16

17

11–13. Nitto Foods Plant, Sagae, Yamagata District, 1963.

11. Additive growth by the multiplication of the structural module.

12. The seasonal character of fruit canning demanded a highly adaptable interior space.

13. The structural provision for growth exploited sculpturally.

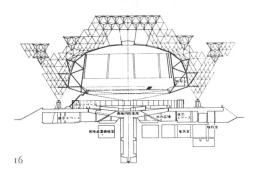

14–17. Toshiba I.H.I. Pavilion, Expo '70, Osaka, 1968–70.

14. Pavilion auditorium raised up on sculptural legs.

15. Section. Auditorium floor platform in raised position.

16. Section. Auditorium floor platform lowered.

17. Structure fabricated from modified Alexander Graham Bell tetrahedral cells.

18

21

19

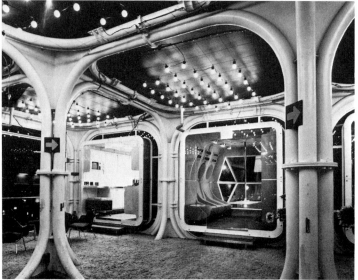

20

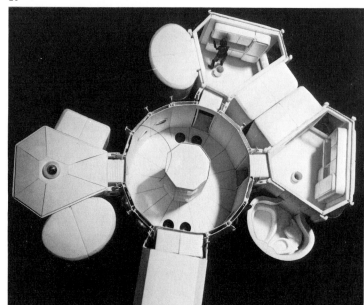

22

18–20. Takara Beautilion, Expo '70, Osaka.
18. Stainless steel capsules 2.2 m wide, 2.2 m high, and 6 m deep inserted in a steel-pipe framework.
19. Space cells grow by the addition of spiculate pipe elements.
20. Interior spaces may be increased or decreased by the addition or subtraction of tubular sections 6m deep.

21–24. Expo '70 housing capsule, Osaka, 1968–70.

73

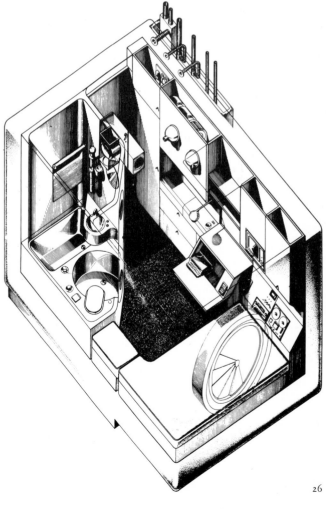

21. Underview of capsule suspended from space
frame roof over the theme zone of Expo '70.
22. View of model showing three capsules clustered
around the information tree and social core.
23. Underside of capsule cluster.
24. Interior of capsule.

25, 26. Business capsule BC-25, Ginza, Tokyo,
1970.
25. View of model. 140 capsules spiral around
two tower cores.
26. Interior of lightweight steel capsule.

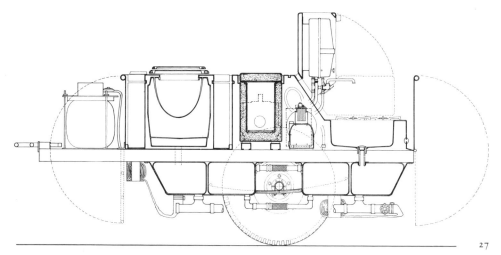

27

28

29

27–29. Moving core MC-18, 1970.
27. Section.
28. View of core services: gas, water closet, shower, refrigerator, water heater, gas range, sink, shower and generator.
29. Service core hitched to prime mover.

30–34. Labour Centre, Nishijin, 1962.
30. South view from street.
31. Board stain ballustrade.
32–34. Plans, bottom to top: first, second and third floor.

30

31

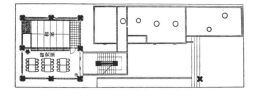

32

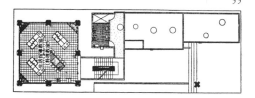

33

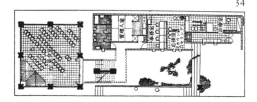

34

35

36

35, 36. Hans Christian Andersen Memorial Hall,
National Children's Land near Yokohama, 1964.
35. Interior.
36. The delicate roof shape evokes traditional
nuances.

37–40. Assembly square and central lodge of
camping area, National Children's Land near
Yokohama, 1964–5.
37, 38. Plans (left to right): lower floor and upper
floor.
39. View at night. The steel tent roof and
mushroom silhouette of the farmers housing in
the earlier agricultural cluster scheme.
40. A varied terrain of steps enlivens the narrow
street.

37

38

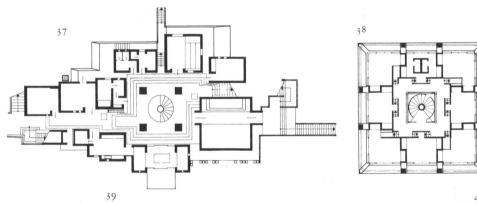

39

40

41

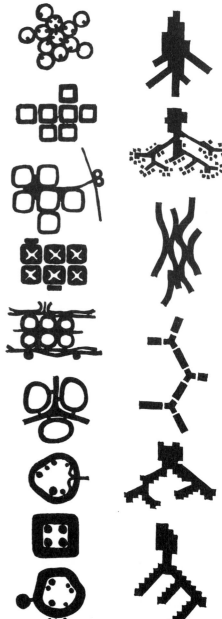

43

42

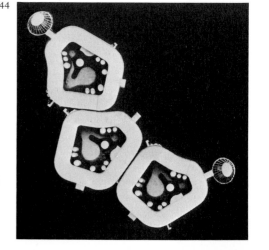

44

41, 42. Honjima Hotel, 1964.
41. Diagonal patterned end wall. View from
south east.
42. Three-storey lounge opens onto longitudinal
corridors.

43. Sketch summary of multiplicative (left) and
additive (right) growth patterns.

45

46

44–46. Yamagata Hawaii Dreamland, 1967.
44. Plan view of model. Metabolic cycles of
multiplicative growth.
45. Focus activity around the interior swimming
court.
44. The outer world is excluded by a medieval
wall and moat.

## Kiyonori Kikutake

At twenty years of age (1948), Kikutake celebrated his degree in architecture from Waseda University by coming second to Kenzo Tange in the competition for the design of the church in the Peace Centre of Hiroshima. Two years later he graduated in engineering, and after forays into the offices of Takenako Co., Murano and Muri, and Motouro Taure's research team at Waseda, he set up in private practice (1953). In 1958, publication of one of his first buildings, the Sky-house, attracted international interest. He was one of the younger panelists at the 1960 World Design Conference in Tokyo and led the formation of the metabolism group.

Kiyonori Kikutake's elaboration of 'Katachi' anticipated Christopher Alexander's investigations into pattern language. The first step in Kikutake's design methodology, the conception of an image of spatial order or 'ka', is the equivalent of Alexander's patterns. In common with other metabolists, Kikutake's form images or patterns are drawn from symbol systems originating in pre-Buddhist Japanese consciousness. This primitive consciousness contained four prototypes which were exhumed and adapted by the metabolists to fit contemporary circumstances: the parallel sacred-symbolic and structural role of the beam and column, the horizontal floor platform and the religious idealization of organic cycles of renewal expressed through architecture and exemplified at Ise.

The sacred 'column of heaven' found in the Izumo and Ise Shrines and preserved as a psychological focus in the sixteenth-century Tea House was exploited by Kikutake for an early series of metabolist proposals. He combined the column/tower theme with a utopian vision of a marine civilization which revitalized the oceanic stream in Japanese consciousness.

Kiyonori Kikutake produced three versions of the marine civilization concept, Marine City (1958), Tower City (1959) and Ocean City (1960, p. 88). The Pacific Hotel at Chigasaki (1966, p. 85) and tower for Expo '70 (p. 89) were pragmatic applications of these ideas. The towers were submerged around a buoyancy ring in Marine City, and in the two later schemes they were mounted on giant floating pontoons (pp. 86, 87). Common to all three projects was the proposal that factory-produced dwelling units should be attached to the surfaces of the cylinders to form vertical cities. Considered in conjunction with his Sky-house (1958, p. 80), these metabolist proposals realized the theoretical distinction between supports and detachable units later described by Nicholas Habraken (1960). The vertical core of open space which penetrates the residential tower of the Pacific Hotel is a survival from the marine tower concept. The bathroom excrescences are vestigial reminders of the detachable living units. Kikutake judiciously incorporated the hotel suites within the depth of the tower wall. The cast aluminium polyhedron capsules, cantilevered from the vertical space frame Landmark Tower at Osaka's Exposition, are a more authentic version of the detachable habitable units.

The Grand Shrine of Izumo (p. 79) was founded in the legendary age, and the mythology surrounding its deity is amongst the most ancient and revered in Japanese history. The existing Shrine buildings possess a powerful aura of primitive simplicity and union with nature. Kikutake chose a tent-like form of space enclosure, not unlike the roof forms of the Ise Shrine buildings. By the simple device of eliminating the conventional wall and converting it into a roof like form, Kikutake created an architectural image deeply evocative of pre-Buddhist architecture. The battered walls, supported by two great pre-stressed concrete ridge beams, consist of a series of pre-cast cills which form narrow horizontal slits, admitting a flood of light to the interior.

*Buildings and Projects*

Design competition for Catholic Cathedral for Peace, Hiroshima, Third Prize (Kenzo Tange Second Prize), 1948
Marine City (Marine civilization), 1958
Mova-block system, 1958
Sky-house, Kikutake Residence, 1958
Tower City (Marine civilization), 1959
Shimane Prefectural Museum, Matsue, 1959
Ocean City (Marine civilization), 1960
Unabara, 1962
Administration Building for Izumo Shrine, Izumo, 1963
Tokoen Hotel, Kaike, Island of Honshu, 1963–4
Pear City, 1965
Pacific Hotel, Chigasaki, Kanagawa Prefecture, 1966
Columbarium, 1966
Miyakonojo Civic Centre, Miyakonojo, 1966
Hagi Civic Centre, Hagi, 1968
Kurume Civic Centre, Kurume, 1968
International competition for the design of low-cost housing, Lima, Peru, First Prize, 1969
Expo Tower, Expo '70, Osaka, 1970

79

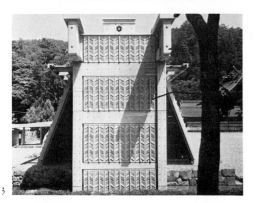

1–3. Administration Building for the Izumo
Shrine, Izumo, 1963.
1. The primitive aura of the Izumo Shrine
permeates Kikutake's building.

2. The battered walls establish a remarkable
inside/outside ambience in the hall interior.
3. View from south. Walls braced against twin
prestressed concrete roof beams.

The Western mind responded to the organic cycle of life, renewal and death with
the fiction of immortality. The Japanese empathy with nature led to a view of life as
a ceaseless flux in which architecture participated. Metabolism is rooted in the native
stream of Japanese architecture pulsing through the open asymmetry of the Katsura
Rikyu, and actively recognized by the periodic rebuilding of the Ise Shrine. Kiyonori Kikutake contends that contemporary change requires a 'changeable, movable
and comprehensive architecture . . . capable of undergoing metabolic changes . . .
we must stop thinking in terms of function and form, and think instead in terms of
space and changeable function . . .'[70] In 1958 he designed his own house, the 'Sky-
house', which consisted of a reinforced concrete living platform supported above the
ground on four sturdy slab columns. Contrary to the C.I.A.M. practice of clustering
services in a central core, Kikutake dispersed them around the periphery of the open
living space to facilitate their future replacement.
According to metabolist theory, the equipment areas, assembled from manufactured
components, are more susceptible to change than the relatively permanent living
areas. The Sky-house exemplifies Habraken's distinction between supports and
detachable units.
The transformation of the traditional horizontal floor platform into a permanent
support or variety of artificial terrain developed from the Sky-house through the

Shimane Prefectural Museum (1959, p. 80) and climaxed in the Miyakonojo City Hall (1966, p. 83). In the Shimane Museum—a typical essay in trabeated concrete—Kikutake clearly defined his building functions, sheltering the two storey museum beneath the superimposed art gallery support structure. The separation of permanent and changeable functions was expressed with dynamic clarity in the Miyakonojo City Hall with its Russian Constructivist bellows-like auditorium shell. The outline and terrain of the concrete platform which houses the lobbies, cafes and seating tiers was envisaged as capable of supporting a range of human uses if for some reason the steel superstructure and equipment were swept away.

The third generation's frustration with monumental static architecture and enquiry into adaptability sustained a variety of dynamic images, varying from Archigram's proposals and Frei Otto's retractable umbrella environments, to Kikutake's occasional experimentation with revolving variable geometry components. The tri-bladed revolving window units which enclose the end walls of the Shimane Museum's art gallery provide a combination of environmental control situations by the ingeniously simple device of making two blades opaque and one transparent. The large horizontal rotating sound boards which Kikutake included in the Kurume civic auditorium (p. 84) provide a measure of acoustic control and spatial subdivision. In a horizontal position, the sound board serves as an acoustic reflector and can be swung into a vertical configuration to double as a space divider when required.

Orthodox functionalism denied the functional ambiguity of many architectural forms. Circulation was considered a type of people-plumbing devoid of social significance. One of the contributions of the third generation has been the realization that circulation provides occasions for valuable informal social intercourse. In the design of the Hagi Civic Centre (p. 82), Kikutake sought to optimize the opportunities for spontaneous social contact through the ambiguous consideration of the interlocking public areas which connect the specialized auditorium and meeting-rooms. The elevated significance of the horizontal civic platform and the subordination of the auditoria to wider social purposes gives meaning to Kikutake's view of architecture as humanistic equipment.

4. Sky-house, Kikutake Residence, Tokyo, 1958. Detachable service units dispersed around the periphery of the open living space.

5–7. Shimane Prefectural Museum, Matsue, 1959.
5. Section. The art gallery bestrides the museum areas.
6. End view. Revolving window elements infil gallery storey.
7. View from garden. An hierarchical rendering of the trabeated motif.

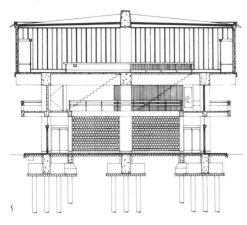

81

8

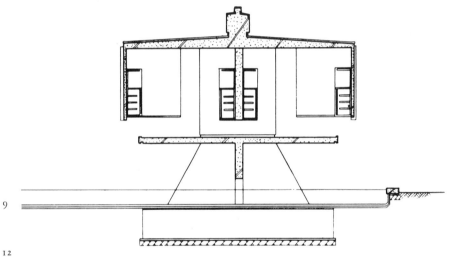

8–12. Columbarium, 1966.
8. Beam and building fuse in an elemental floating image.
9. Cross section. Levitation explained.
10. Longitudinal section.
11. Floor plan.
12. End view.

9

12

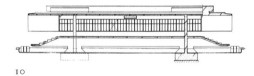

10

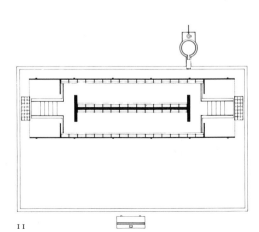

11

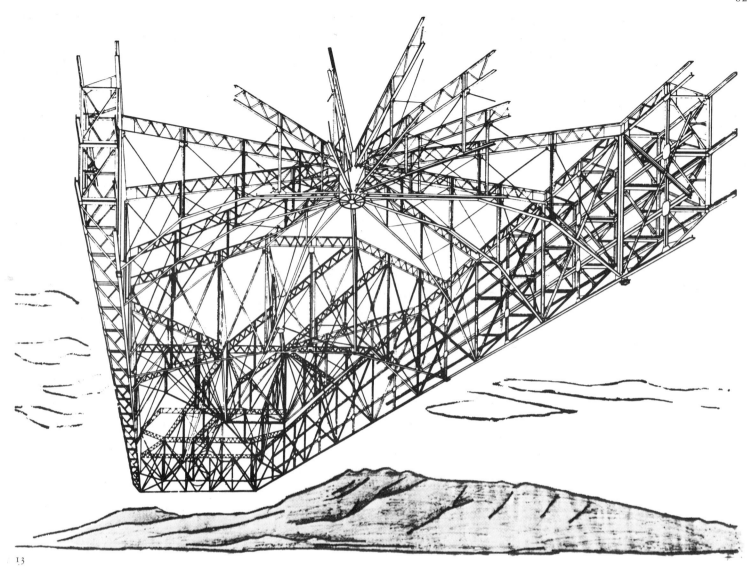

13

14

15

16

17

18

13–15. Hagi Civic Centre, Hagi, 1968.
13. Sketch of the disembodied space frame roof canopy.
14. View from south east. Bipartite façade theme.
15. Small hall viewed from the lobby. The interior is dominated by the lightweight roof framing.

16–19. Miyakonojo City Hall, Miyakonojo, 1966.
16. View from north west.
17. View from west. The separation of permanent and changeable functions is expressed by the dualism of platform and roof.
18. Auditorium interior.
19. Section.

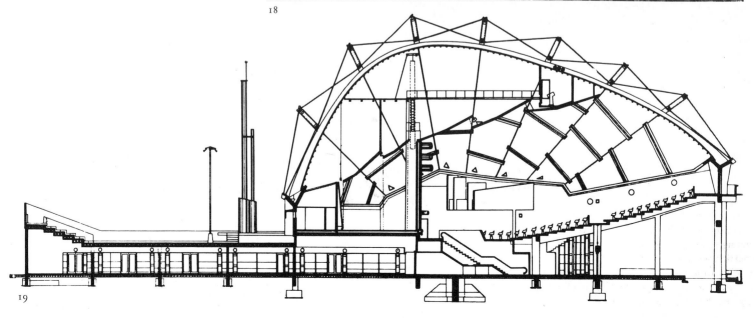

19

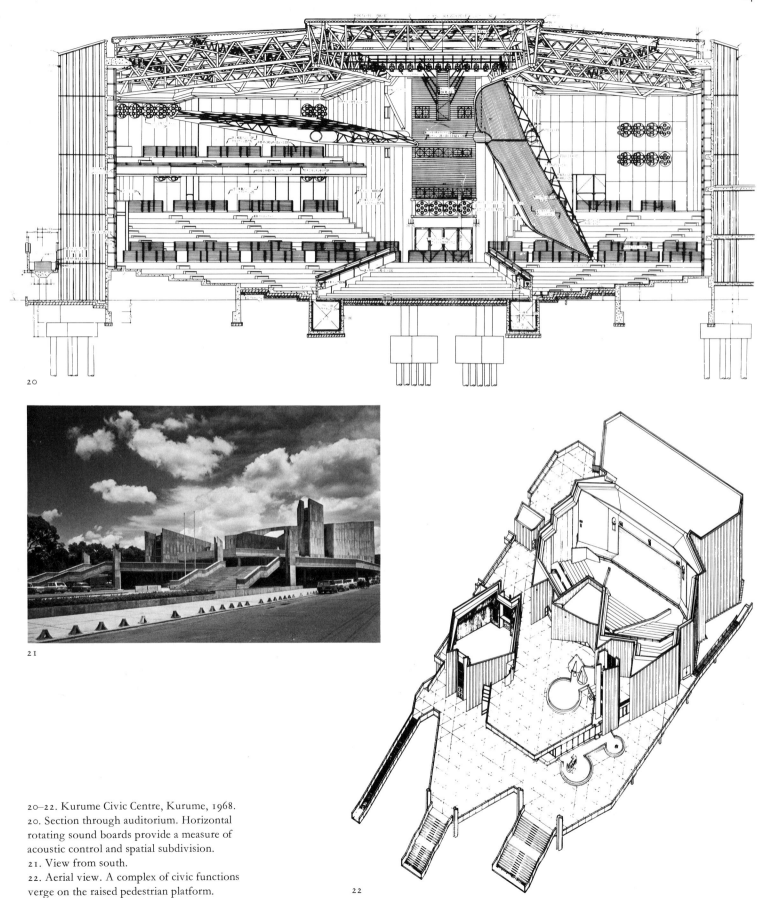

20

21

22

20–22. Kurume Civic Centre, Kurume, 1968.
20. Section through auditorium. Horizontal
rotating sound boards provide a measure of
acoustic control and spatial subdivision.
21. View from south.
22. Aerial view. A complex of civic functions
verge on the raised pedestrian platform.

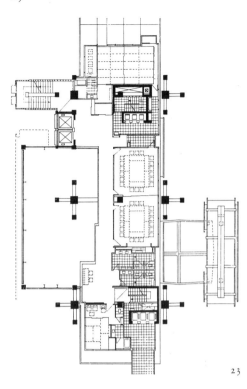

23, 24. Tokoen Hotel, Kaike, Island of Honshu, 1963–4.
23. Plan, mezzanine floor.
24. View from east.

25, 26. Pacific Hotel, Chigasaki, Kanagawa Prefecture, 1966.
25. Bathroom pods cantilever from the seven-sided tower façade.
26. Plan, second floor. The open vertical core space is similar to Kikutake's marine tower schemes.

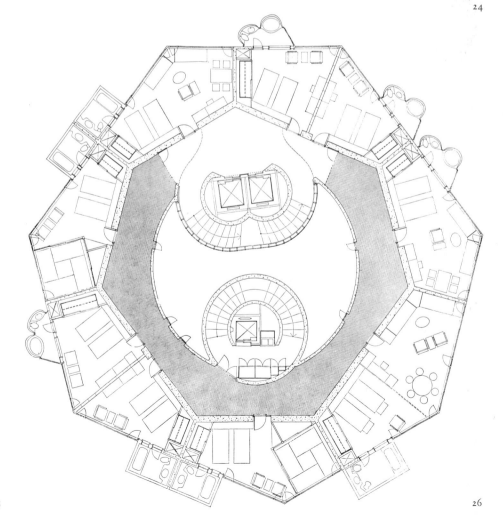

27. Marine civilization scheme, 1960.
View of model showing the residential towers at different stages of growth on artificial island.
28. Unabara, 1962.
Spherical floats support an artificial island from which extend submarine cylinders with 'clipped on' living capsules.
29. Sketch of marine civilization.

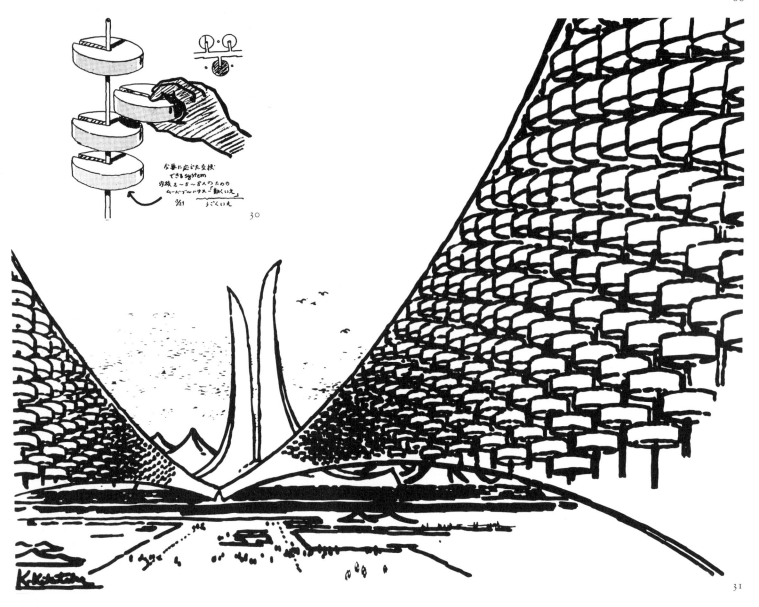

30

31

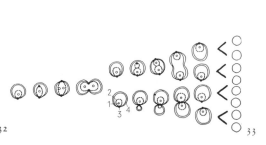

30. Mova-block system to permit change, 1958.

31. Ocean City, 1960.
A crushing image of urban order which negates the individual.

32. Unabara, 1962.
View of model.

33. Diagrammatic application of the biological phenomenon of cell fission to the problem of urban growth. Key: 1 control tower, 2 housing ring, 3 administration block, 4 production ring.

32

33

35

34, 35. Expo Tower, Expo '70, Osaka, 1970.
34. Night view from south.
35. Cast aluminium polyhedron capsules from the tower space frame.

34

## Arata Isozaki

The two most important influences on Arata Isozaki's architecture were Kenzo Tange and the City of Oita on the island of Kyushu. Isozaki was born at Oita in 1931, and the city honoured its former son by monopolizing his architectural services. Following his graduation from the Department of Architecture at Tokyo University in 1954, Isozaki joined Kenzo Tange's research staff while completing an M. A. in 1956 and a Ph. D. in 1961. Both Tange and Isozaki gained from their close association (1954–61). The influence of Isozaki's ideas is clearly apparent in the plan for Tokyo which Tange prepared in 1960. In 1963, he established his own office, the Arata Isozaki Atelier. However, he collaborated closely with Kenzo Tange on the Festival Plaza for Expo '70 at Osaka.

In the decade of the sixties, Arata Isozaki encompassed the contradictory architectural ideals of form and antiform. The cultivation of antithetical concepts as a source of philosophic truth is a feature of the Japanese intellectual tradition and may explain the ease of Isozaki's conversion equally as well as the insinuation of a light-fingered eclecticism. The Expo '70 Festival Plaza (pp. 98, 99) appropriated Cedric Price's investigation of servicing as an alternative to monumental form in the Fun Palace Project for Joan Littlewood (1961). The technological sophistication of the Festival Plaza equipment was far in advance of anything envisaged by Price. It revealed the specialized application and high cost of intensively serviced environments.

Relative to Kikutake, Arata Isozaki's inclusion of traditional patterns in his form images is more explicit and forceful. The firepower of the Oita Prefectural Library (p. 94) is equivalent to a heavy battle cruiser. The Spatial (1960) and Space (1962) City Schemes (p. 91) announced his pronounced obsession with the beam and post motif. Isozaki transformed the beam from a structural member of somewhat overblown proportions into the sole element of enclosure by a process of architectural osmosis.

The Spatial City proposal consisted of an interlocking system of spatial co-ordinates based on a grid of vertical service towers and connecting beams which engorged the architectural space. The ambiguous imagery of the vertical towers was reminiscent of traditional wood posts and petroleum cracking-towers. A similar system was incorporated in the overland sector of Tange's plan for Tokyo on which Isozaki assisted. The plan created living space by the expedient of an interlocking system of beams supported high above the ground on vertical service towers. Tange implemented the concept in his Yamanashi Press and Radio Centre at Kofu (1967).

In the Space City aerial clusters for the renewal of a section of Tokyo, Isozaki blew up the traditional column and bracket structural device climaxed in the south gate of the Todaiji at Nara (1181) from an architectural to a superhuman urban scale which dwarfed the existing city. The elaborate ten-tier system of brackets in the Todaiji leap frog thirty feet out into space and support a massive roof overhang. Isozaki inserted plug-in house capsules between the cantilevered brackets. Tange's Shizuoka building, Ginza (1967), is a modified version of the idea.

Huddled along a two kilometre strip of his home city, Oita, five buildings—the Medical Hall (1959–60), Iwata Gakuen High School (1963–4, p. 93), N's Residence (1964) the Prefectural Library (1964–6, p. 94) and the Fukuoka Mutual Bank (1966–7, p. 95)—record Isozaki's preoccupation with a sculptural interpretation of architecture. Like Paul Rudolph, Isozaki combines an orderly, geometrical plan and free open cross-section. He seeks to produce unexpected and impressive spaces by exploiting contrasts of height, scale, and changes of level. Something of the feeling

*Buildings and Projects*

of James Stirling's Leicester University Building (pp. 136–7) intrudes in the tower form and forty-five degree alignment of the skylights in the Fukuoka Mutual Bank. Isozaki's involvement with the tactile sensuous aspects of form leads to an intensification of the physical experience of form and surface. He saturated the interior of the Fukuoka Mutual Bank with pure colours—cobalt blue, red, yellow, orange, green and pink—according to his concept of space colour. The space resonances of colour considered in environmental terms can enhance spatial character and intensify the architectural experience.

Isozaki heightens the atmospheric drama and freshness of his interior forms by the soft play of natural daylight beamed from ingeniously situated skylights.

The devastating sweep of the concrete cannons which straddle the Oita Prefectural Library is out of all proportion to its modest superstructure. The programme called for a library to accommodate 200,000 volumes, reading areas and a small auditorium. The library is organized around a two-storeyed core formed by parallel double walls which enclose the browsing area. Both the Iwata Gakuen High School and Fukuoka Mutual Bank were given central circulation spines which perform a similar role to the deep-gorged browsing area. A series of spaced hollow concrete beams which carry the air-conditioning ducts span these rooms and are supported on their

1. Spatial City montage, 1960.
The new megastructure rising out of the ruins of the past preserves the tectonic motif of beam and column.

2. Space City aerial clusters, 1962, mime the elaborate column brackets of traditional Japanese carpentry.

extremities by free-standing transverse beams. Inverted 'U' beams, closed at their ends to simulate the smaller tubular beams, complete the roof deck.

The library interior was assembled from a complex interplay of contrasting spaces. The tall browsing area overflows at either end into related one-storey rooms. Changes of floor level and ceiling height and adventurous sky-lighting heighten the sculptural quality of the spaces. In the reading area next door, the space is less eventful, low, expansive and horizontal. Isozaki delights in unexpected and sometimes arbitrary spatial effects as a means of enhancing the expressive quality of his interiors. The application of pure colour on burlap wall surfaces contrasts with the grey toughness of the building exterior.

Among the younger Japanese architects, Isozaki was the first to establish personal contact with Archigram. Their infectious sense of fun invaded his Fukuoka Mutual Bank at Oita. The citizens showed their approval of Isozaki's uninhibited essay in pop sculpture by increasing their patronage. A blind splayed tower surmounts the exposed corner of the banking chamber, from where a suspended pedestrian bridge makes its diagonal crossing. Strip skylights infil between the forty-five degree opposed ribs and attach to the structural spine which follows the alignment of the pedestrian flyway. Set at right angles to the skylight pattern parallel cranked beams, similar to the library podium cladding, provide a transition in scale from the lofty banking chamber to the low entrance foyers. Contrary to the prevailing conservative, middle-minded banking image, Isozaki imported a youthful exuberance, daringly expressed by an abundance of bright colour.

The Festival Plaza at Expo '70 was conceived by Kenzo Tange as a third generation happening, a coming-of-age celebration hosted by Japan. As if in confirmation, Christopher Alexander, Moshe Safdie, Archigram, Yona Friedman, and Noriaki Kurokawa were invited to contribute exhibits to be suspended in the plaza roof. And although the giant space-frame roof failed to de-materialize into an Utzonite cloud, it clearly demonstrated Tange's anti-architecture intentions.

Archigram, in particular, publicized the ideal of an architecture which interferes as little as possible with the exercise of human freedom and spontaneous action. The pop festivals typified by Woodstock were a major inspiration. Such a permissive affirmation of individual values relegated architecture to the status of a disposable environmental utility. The Monaco Entertainments Centre (pp. 110–11) is the closest Archigram has come to realizing the proposition. The Festival Plaza which Isozaki produced cashiered a number of Archigram favourites such as the robot and mobile environmental gadgetry, and employed them on a scale and at a level of technological sophistication which rivalled even the most way-out Archigram proposals. In a sense, the Festival Plaza tested the Archigram philosophy within a specific set of parameters and showed the high cost of freedom.

The Plaza was intended by Tange 'to be a space of spontaneity, not one where sponsors alone would have complete control, but a place where the audience too can participate . . . a space without a fixed form is all that is needed, but in practical planning it first became important to provide the shelter of a roof . . .'[71]

The multiple uses of the plaza required that the seating, environmental and mechanical equipment possess sufficient flexibility and mobility to accommodate and service any one of the possible activities and festivities. These activities were of three main types: formal national day festivities, resting and informal social intercourse, and elaborate large scale pageants and shows. Isozaki sought to promote the plaza deck as a place of simultaneous swelling movement similar in feeling to the surging eventfulness captured in the paintings of Piet Bruegel. The light and sound equipment and the large set pieces were trundled around on mobile trolleys running along the underside of the roof space-frame. They were supplemented at ground

93

3

level by a complex array of mobile units which included stages, dressing rooms, sets, seating and even a data gathering robot with moving trunk and arms. The co-ordination of all this equipment for simultaneous performances necessitated an elaborate, computerized control system with the possibility of independent local activity through a sub-control station.

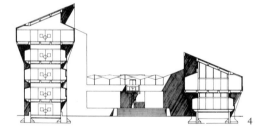

4

3–5. Iwata Gakuen High School, Oita, Kyushu, 1963–4.
3. General view.
4. Section.
5. Plan. Towers linked by elevated pedestrian decks.

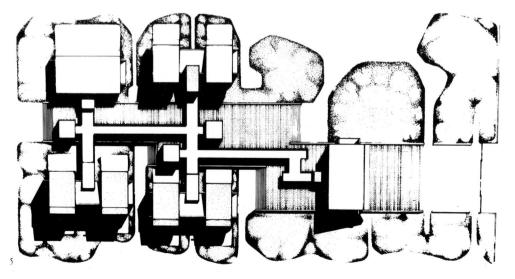

5

6

7

6–9. Prefectural Library, Oita, Kyushu, 1964–6.
6. A stepped mastaba leads across an abutting bridge to the two-storey central zone.

7. The south face, a *tour de force* of concrete cannons.
8. Section through north wing.
9. Axonometric drawing of the roof log-jam.

8

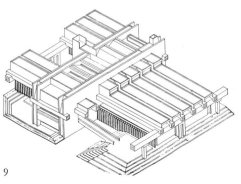

9

10–13. Fukuoka Mutual Bank, Oïta, Kyushu, 1966–7.
10. East elevation.
11. Aerial view of model showing roof structure.

12. Axonometric sketch of main banking chamber interior.
13. View of main banking chamber penetrated by pedestrian bridge and lit by forty-five degree roof lights.

11

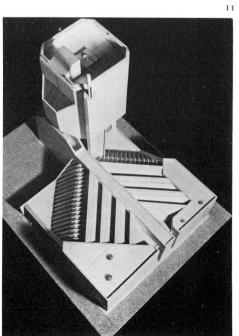

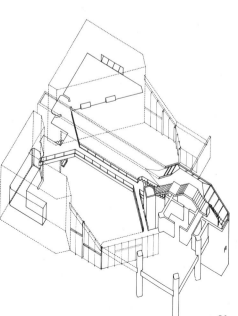

13

12

14

14–17. Skopje Reconstruction Plan, Kenzo
Tange Team, 1965–6.
14. City gate, view from west, first phase.
15. Multilevel system of traffic junctions transform express traffic into local traffic.
16. City gate, view from north west.
17. City image.

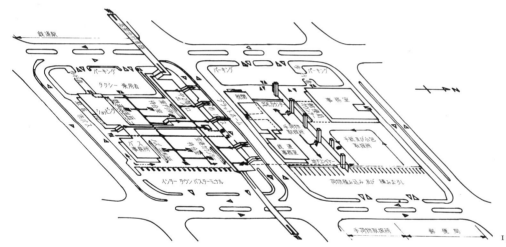

15

16

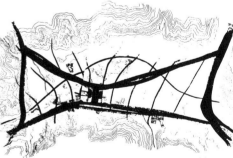

17

97

18, 19. Electric Labyrinth, 14th Triennale Milan, 1968.
18. Axonometric of revolving panels which serve as projection surfaces for electric media.
19. Light image environment.

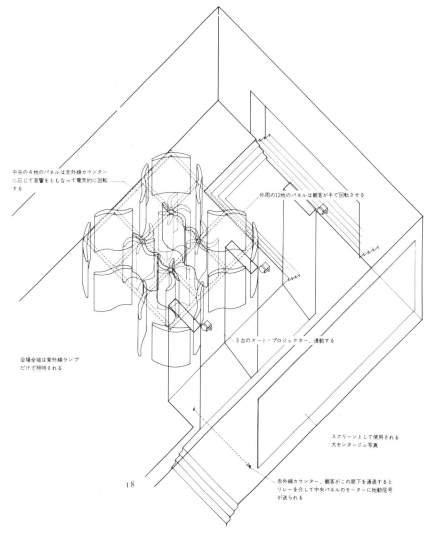

中央の4枚のパネルは赤外線カウンターに応じて音響をともなって電気的に回転する

外周の12枚のパネルは観客が手で回転させる

3台のオート・プロジェクター，連動する

会場全域は紫外線ランプだけで照明される

スクリーンとして使用される大モンタージュ写真

赤外線カウンター，観客がこの廊下を通過するとリレーを介して中央パネルのモーターに始動信号が送られる

18

19

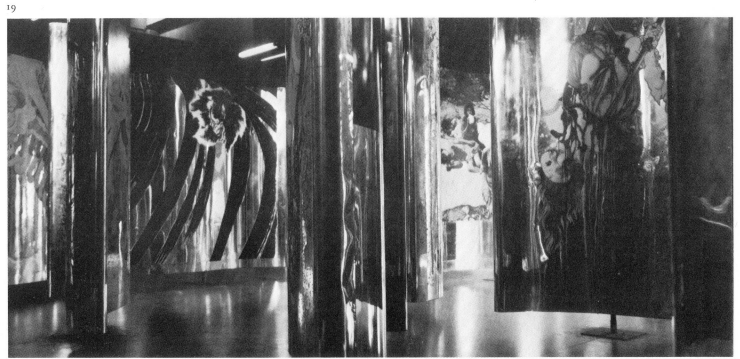

20

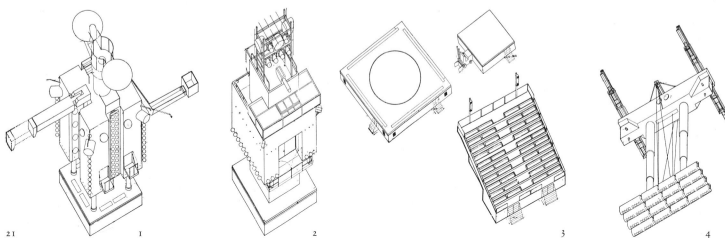

21        1             2                   3                 4

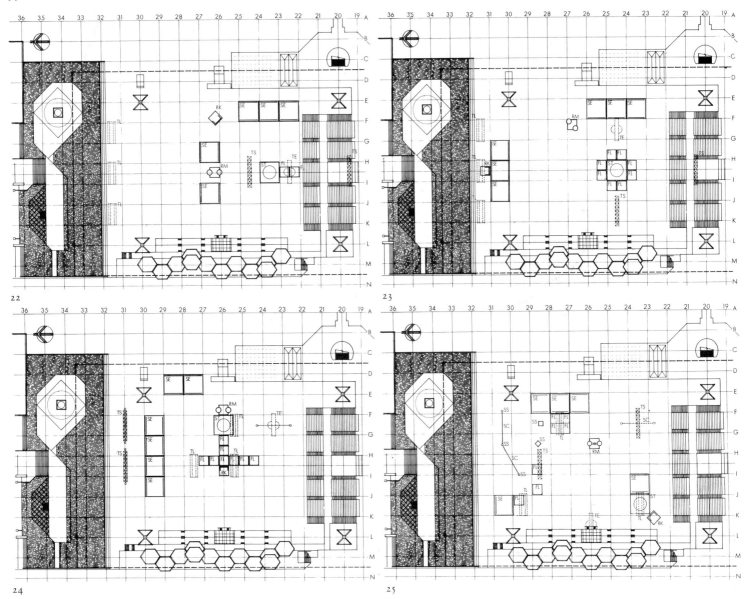

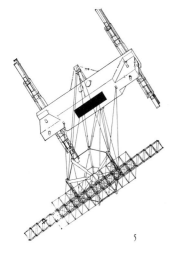

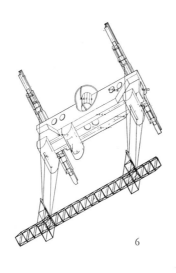

20–25. Festival Plaza, Expo '70, Osaka, 1968–70.
20. View of model.
21. Mechanical equipment: 1 performance robot RM, 2 subcontrol station RK, 3 movable stage ST, wagon stage WS, movable seats SE, 4 lighting booth trolley TL, 5 stage setting trolley TS, 6 stage controlling trolley TE.
22–25. Plans showing alternative equipment dispositions.

26

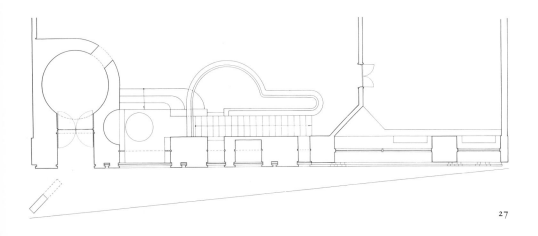

27

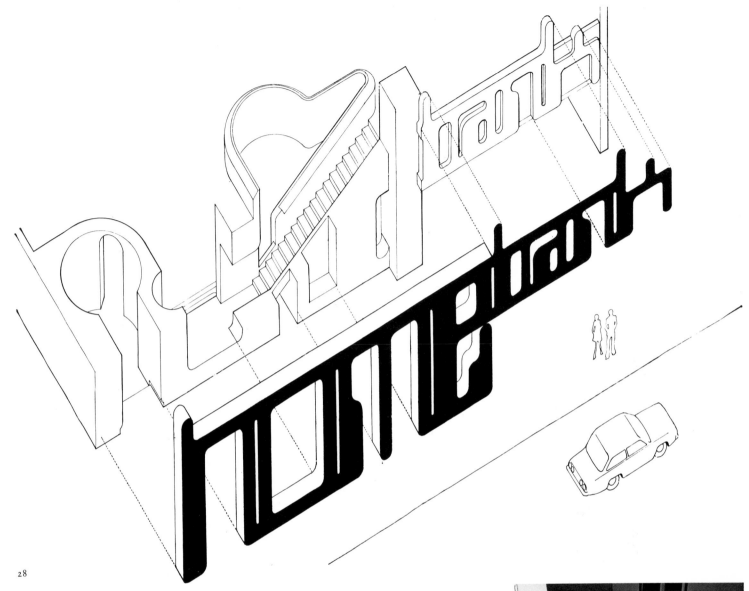

28

29

26–29. Fukuoka Mutual Bank, Tokyo Branch,
1970–1.
26. Night and day street front.
27. Plan.
28. Axonometric.
29. View of stair, nostalgic early modern interior
with colour space.

# Archigram

Archigram is a fluid association of individuals; a sort of 'multi-coloured umbrella held by sleight of hand' and united by common interests and antipathies. Around a nucleus consisting of Peter Cook (b. 1936), Warren Chalk (b. 1927), Ron Herron (b. 1930), Dennis Crompton (b. 1935), Mike Webb (b. 1937) and David Greene (b. 1937), other people spontaneously join-in and drop-out. The group coalesced from a series of chance encounters and purposeful introductions. Peter Cook, Mike Webb and David Greene put Archigram 1 together in 1961. Later in the same year, Peter Cook invited three friends, Ron Herron, Warren Chalk and Dennis Crompton, all employed in the special works branch of the London County Council design team for the South Bank Arts Centre (1967) to contribute to later Archigram productions. The two groups were united as members of a design team formed by Theo Crosby for the redevelopment of Euston Station a year later. In 1963, they collaborated on the 'Living City' Exhibition for the Institute of Contemporary Arts, which crystallized in the Archigram philosophy. Although the original team now teaches in England and America, they managed to provide the winning scheme in the international competition for the design of an entertainments centre at Monte Carlo which promises 'a place in the sun' for Archigram.

A striking parallel exists between Archigram's interest in Russian Constructivism and their affinity with another equally Russian movement, Nihilism. In essence, Archigram denies the value of disciplined authoritarian systems of imposed environmental order. They contend that any order as such should crystallize from spontaneous interactions within the environmental system. This is a more extreme manifestation of the third generation search for intrinsic environmental patterns of order. Their schemes minimize the architect's power for shaping the environment and aims instead at fostering the active democratic forces of participation and involvement. The design problem consists of two exercises: the decomposition of the context into a hierarchy of requirements, and their resolution in terms of a set of patterns which must be reconstituted as a complete whole form. Christopher Alexander concentrated on the first stage of analysis, while Archigram have devoted themselves to the second. Moreover, the success of pattern-matching depends on the availability of a large reservoir of pattern material drawn from contemporary experience. Peter Cook clarified Archigram's intentions with the statement: 'We are in the cataloguing business, and our work is that of illuminating and *extending* and *reinventing* the catalogue.'[72]

Consideration of the two fundamental objections has caused Archigram to be dismissed as a 'kookie pop art frivol' (to quote Banham). Their critics assert with some justification that their choice of subject matter is largely irrelevant to the purposes and means of architecture, their insights into advanced technology trivial, and their contribution to the refinement of building technique negligible. By foregoing the preliminary systematic analysis of real problems, they have robbed their pattern development of any significance for architecture. Archigram's technological and science fiction fantasies do not represent real knowledge about the environment or technology any more than *Art Nouveau* is a source of botanical insights. *Art Nouveau* and Archigram are the products of a similar process and both utilize visual metaphors to create pattern systematizations of form. This is intuitive art. Archigram's accumulation of a large body of pattern material inspired by contemporary experience provides an important source of patterns for use by designers seeking to make the leap from programme to form. The fresher these patterns are, the greater their value in terms of experience. Archigram's random pattern explorations are a

*Buildings and Projects*

Furniture Manufacturers Association Building, High Wycombe. Michael Webb, 1959
Sin Centre for Leicester Square. Michael Webb, 1961
Living City Exhibition, Institute of Contemporary Arts, London
City Interchange. Warren Chalk and Ron Herron, 1963
Mound—a city terminal redevelopment. Peter Cook, 1964
Exhibition Tower for Montreal. Peter Cook, 1964
Computer City. Dennis Crompton, 1964
Walking Cities. Ron Herron, 1964
Plug-in City. Peter Cook, 1964
Plug-in Tower. Warren Chalk, 1964
Plug-in University Node. Peter Cook, 1965
The Gasket Capsule. Ron Herron and Warren Chalk, 1965
The Living Pod. David Greene, 1966
Cushicle. Michael Webb, 1966
Control and Choice. Group project, 1967
Suitaloon. Michael Webb, 1968
Manzak. Ron Herron, 1969
Monaco Entertainments Centre, Monte Carlo. Peter Cook, Colin Fournier, David Greene, Ron Herron, Ken Allison, Tony Rickaby, 1969
Instant City. Ron Herron, 1969–70
Bournemouth Steps, 1970

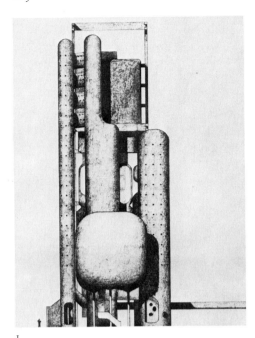

1

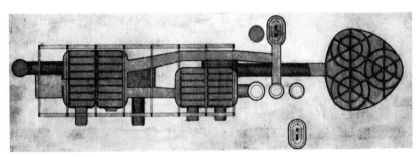

2

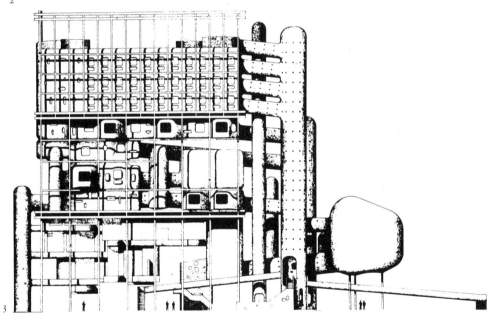

3

1–3. Furniture Manufacturers Association Building, High Wycombe. Project: Michael Webb, 1959.
1. End elevation.
2. Plan.
3. Front elevation.

valuable contribution to third-generation consciousness. Their very ambiguity and lack of explicitness assures them of a multi-valent flexibility and capacity to survive beyond the immediate present. Until design can be simplified to a purely rational activity, the intuitive approach as exemplified by Archigram will remain an essential feature of the creative process. Warren Chalk confirms: 'We are not trying to make houses like cars, cities like oil refineries, even if we seem to be . . . this analogous imagery . . . will eventually be digested into a creative system . . . Yet it has become necessary to extend ourselves into such disciplines *in order to discover an appropriate language to the present-day situation*.[73] (authors italics)

A more serious objection is that Archigram accepts the basic technology and assumptions of a consumer society. If that society proves to be non-sustainable, then Archigram's imagery will become obsolete.

An important influence on Archigram theory was the advent and success of con-

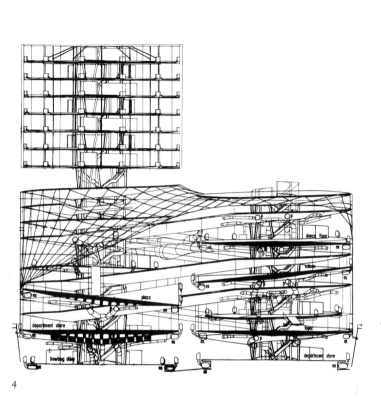

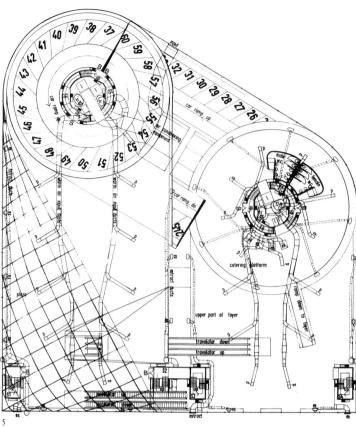

4, 5. Sin Centre for Leicester Square. Project:
Michael Webb, 1961.
4. Section, mechanical services determine the
environmental character.
5. Plan. Floor ramps spiral around two service
cores from which the tentacle-like air ducts spread
out.

sumer-related production and services. Architecture compares unfavourably with
consumer technology in the degree to which it subordinates the building user to
formal aesthetic concerns. Beginning with ideas of flow, movement and expendability, Archigram moved on to metamorphoses, change, plug-in and at a later stage to
consumer choice, freedom and individual emancipation.

The growth of service industries attracted Archigram's attention and reinforced the
concept of Architecture as servicing people. A close friend of the group, Cedric
Price, suggested the idea of servicing as an alternative to architecture. His idea was
to construct an environment flexible enough to be immediately responsive to the individual. He imagined a type of non-building which would liberate man from the
constraints of monumental building.

The flux of ideas in the decade of the sixties arising from a common experience provided the raw material for Archigram's iconography. A number of the ideas
emerged independently of, and in isolation from, the Archigram group. Examples
of such ideas would be variable geometry responsive structures, mobile life supports, capsule housing and the kit of parts. A prevalent response was the dematerial-
ization of structure through an increasing emphasis on mechanical services as the
prime means of creating a habitable environment. Archigram was inspired by life to
create a new range of environments in which architecture was envisaged as infinite
and transient. The building user was conceived of as a consumer, and architecture
was restructured to investigate ways in which the possibilities of choice and participation could be enhanced.

Although Archigram has had few opportunities to build, the group has been re-
sponsible for numerous national and international exhibitions. These exposures of
Archigram ideas have provided important opportunities to develop and test their
theories against the public response. In retrospect, Archigram's success in winning

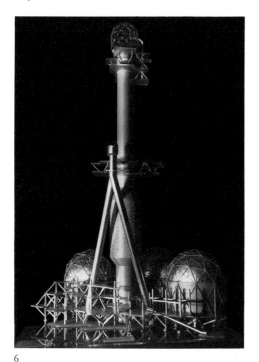

the international competition for the design of the Monaco Entertainments Centre (1969, pp. 110–11) is hardly surprising. The direction of their thinking, focusing on multi-use, mobility and servicing, was an intense preparation for the solution of the problems posed by the requirements of the entertainments centre.

At Monte Carlo, Archigram dug the entertainments centre into the ground and pulled the earth back over a great concrete dome. The competition programme had specified that the centre should provide facilities for circus, ice hockey, banquet, variety shows and cultural events. The designers developed a 'features kit' of mechanical servicing robots, capsules and mobile supports. Permutations of the kit of parts provide the necessary functional flexibility within a physically defined environment. Arata Isozaki implemented a considerably more sophisticated version of the concept at Osaka, including the robot idea which realized even Archigram's most extravagant science fiction fantasies. Archigram's relaxed assurance and insistence that architecture is fun imbues their designs with a rare gaiety and humour.

6

6–8. Exhibition Tower for Montreal. Project: Peter Cook, 1964.
6. View of model shows affinities with gas tanks and petrol cracking towers.
7. Section.
8. Plan, base area level +71.

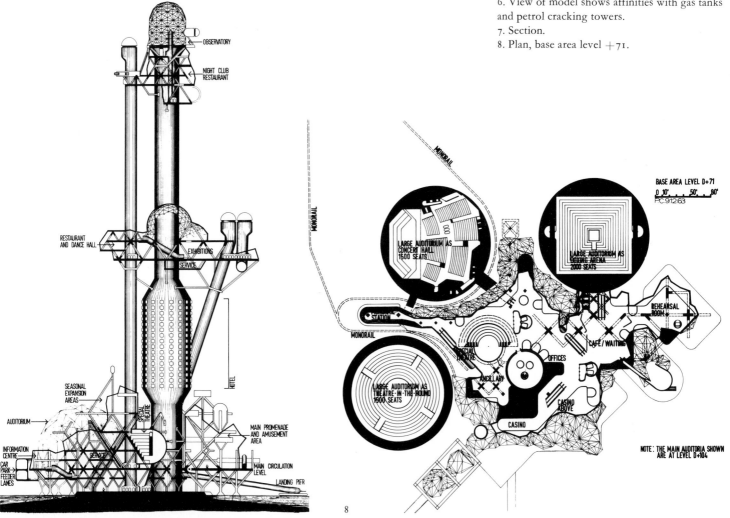

7

8

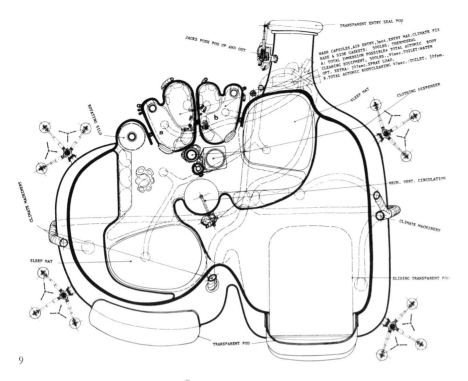

TRANSPARENT ENTRY SEAL POD

JACKS PUSH POD UP AND OUT

WASH CAPSULES,AIR ENTRY,3pnt.ENTRY MAX.CLIMATE FIX
BASE & SIDE GASKETS: 5OOLBS. THERMOSEAL
A: TOTAL IMMERSION POSSIBLE+ TOTAL AUTOMIC BODY
CLEANING EQUIPMENT, 5OOLBS.,95sec.TOILET:WATER
OPT. EXTRA: 107sec.SPRAY LOAD.
B.TOTAL AUTOMIC BODYCLEANING 97sec.:TOILET: 10fpm.

SLEEP MAT

CLOTHING DISPENSER

ROTATING SILO

a

b

MECH. VERT. CIRCULATION

CLIMATE MACHINERY

CLIMATE MACHINERY

SLEEP MAT

SLIDING TRANSPARENT POD

TRANSPARENT POD

9

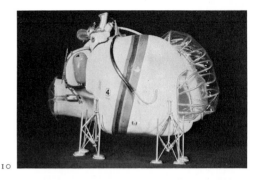

10

11

9–11. The Living Pod. Project: David Greene, 1966.
9. Plan, fully applianced house.
10. View of model.
11. Interior view of model.

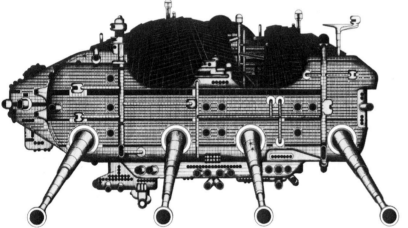

12, 13. Walking Cities. Project: Ron Herron, 1964.
12. Elevation.
13. New York montage.

12

13

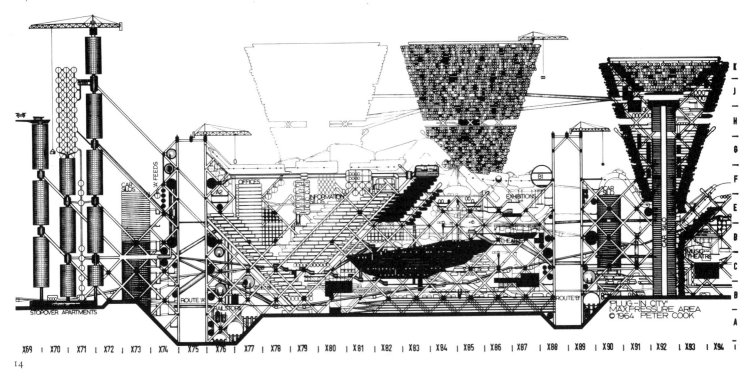

STOPOVER APARTMENTS · ROUTE 'A' · ROUTE 'B' · PLUG-IN CITY MAX PRESSURE AREA © 1964 PETER COOK

| X69 | X70 | X71 | X72 | X73 | X74 | X75 | X76 | X77 | X78 | X79 | X80 | X81 | X82 | X83 | X84 | X85 | X86 | X87 | X88 | X89 | X90 | X91 | X92 | X93 | X94 |

14

14–16. Plug-in City, maximum pressure area.
Project: Peter Cook, 1964.
14. Section.
15. Section. Megastructure incorporating lifts, service tubes and throw-away living capsules.
16. Axonometric of local district, medium pressure area.

16

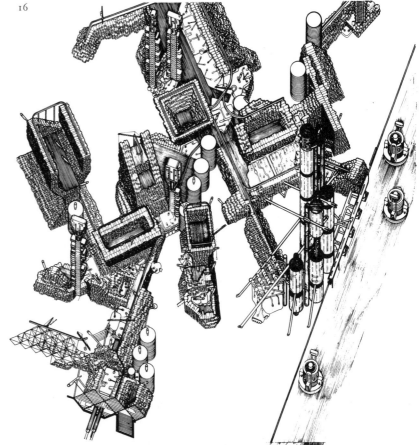

15

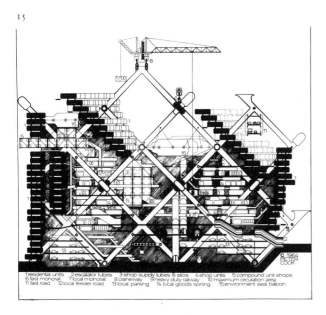

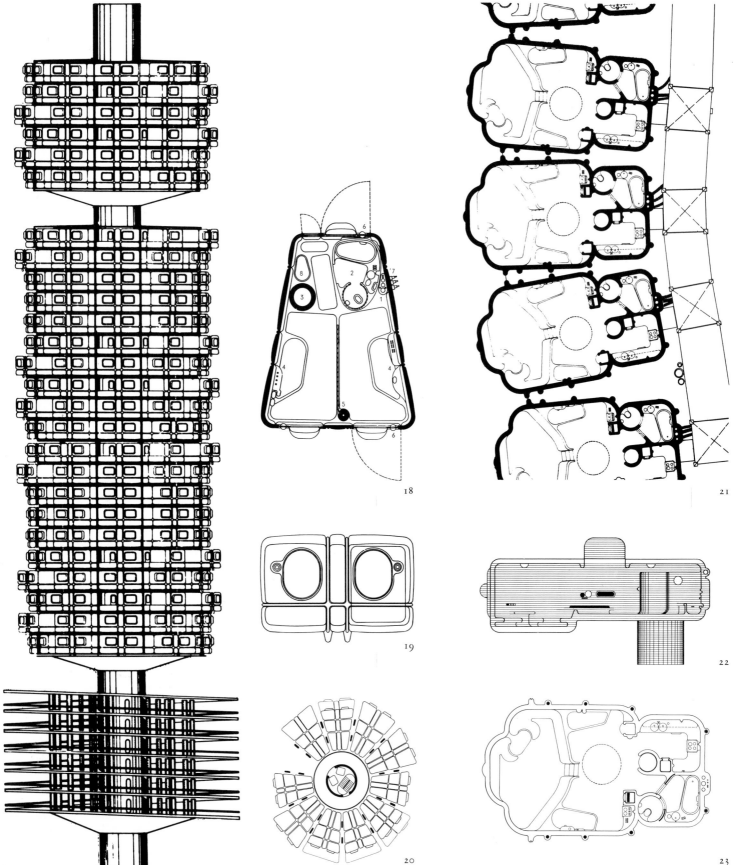

17

18

19

20

21

22

23

17–20. Plug-in Tower. Project: Warren Chalk, 1964.
17. Elevation.
18. Plan of capsule. Key: 1 service duct, 2 kitchen or bathroom, 3 pneumatic lift, 4 clip-on appliance wall, 5 spring-loaded divider, 6 wide service door, 7 services connection, 8 storage unit.
19. Capsule exterior face.
20. Plan. Capsule attachment to tower core containing vertical circulation.

21–23. The Gasket Capsule. Project: Ron Herron and Warren Chalk, 1965.
21. Horizontal servicing of the capsules along an umbilical conveyor belt.
22. Section.
23. Plan.

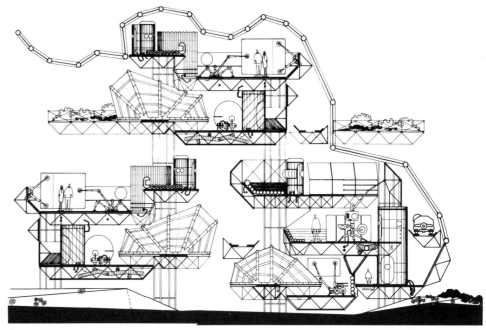

24

a Communications system input and visual system output
b Power cell
c Audio input
d Suit support pads
e Upper support frame
f Suit communications system memory and control
k Floor panel supports
h Power plug for connexion with suited riders and other living envelopes

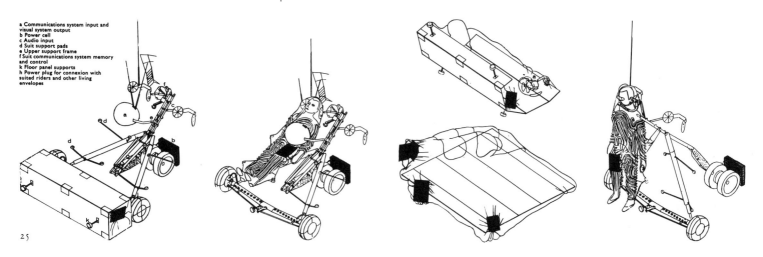

25

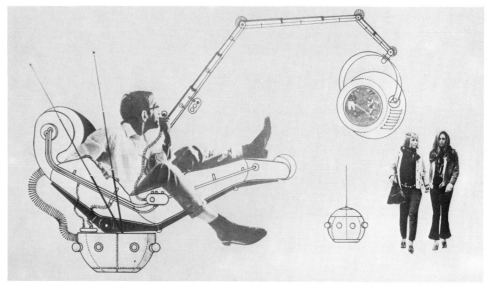

26

24. Control and Choice. Group project, 1967. Open network with adjustable walls, service robots, electric cars contained by a movable pneumatic envelope.

25. Suitaloon. Project: Michael Webb, 1968. Clothing is architecture metaphor inspired by the environmental sophistication of space suits.

26. Manzak montage. Project: Ron Herron, 1969. Servicing and furniture concept.

27

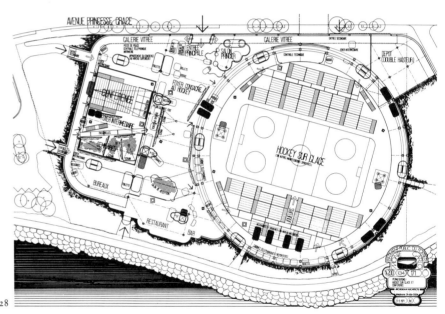

28

27–32. Monaco Entertainments Centre, Monte
Carlo. Competition. Architects: Peter Cook,
Colin Fournier, David Greene, Ron Herron, Ken
Allison and Tony Rickaby with Frank Newby as
consulting engineer, 1969.
27. Diagrammatic section.
28. Plan. Servicing kit deployed for combined ice
hockey and conference event.
29. Plan. Servicing kit deployed for circus variety
spectacle.
30. Site plan. Entertainments centre dome buried
below earth mound.
31. Montage of ice hockey event.
32. Montage of circus event.

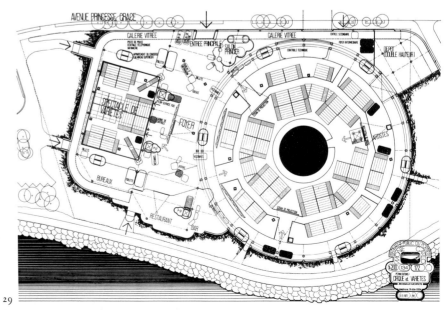

29

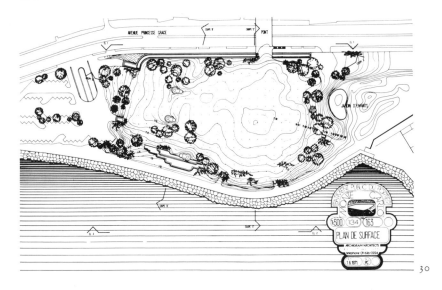

30

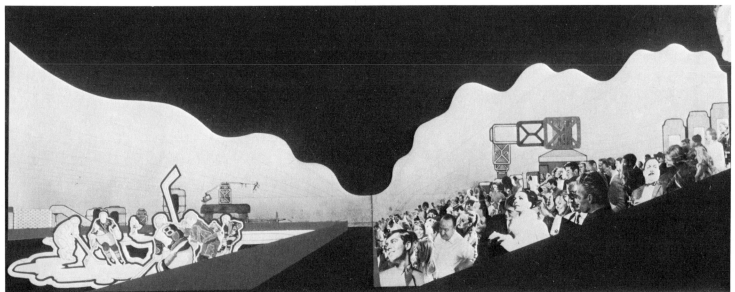

31

32

33

34

33–36. Instant City at the seaside. Project: Ron Herron, 1969–70.

33. Montage, 1969.

34. Section. Deployed for an event, left to right: restaurant and cabaret, dancing, exhibition and play area, light-sound response tents, television screens, balloon tower, ice rink, music dome, show ring and revolving bars.

35. Local parts. Montage, 1970. Location: Market towns and villages.

36. Plan of Instant City deployed for an event.

35

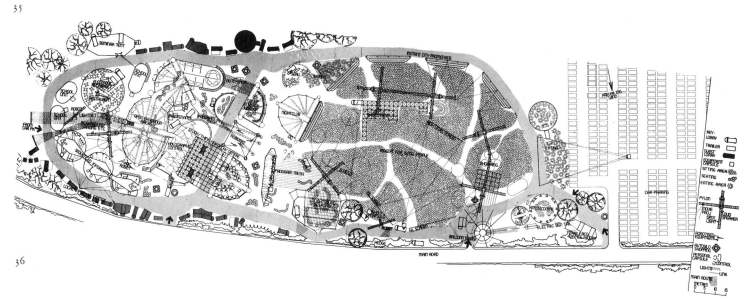

36

# Frei Otto

Born into a family of woodcarvers and sculptors in 1925, Frei Otto was at first apprenticed as a stonemason. However, the Second World War intervened, and after serving as a pilot, he commenced his architectural studies at the Berlin Technical University (1948–52). The publication of his doctoral thesis on suspension roofs (1954) was followed eight years later by an important book on pneumatic structures which aroused considerable interest in the idea. The architectural centre which he established at Berlin served as a model for the Institute for Lightweight Structures which he subsequently founded at Stuttgart University (1959). A close collaboration with manufacturers, especially the famous tent-maker Peter Stromeyer, leavened Frei Otto's theoretical orientation with a working knowledge of techniques and material performance. Frei Otto benefited from design partnerships with other architects such as Rolf Gutbrod and Kenzo Tange, who lent a sense of space, organization and planning which complemented his own structural expertise. He widened the third-generation's repertoire of structural techniques and showed the value of a logical expression of structure.

The survival of architecture in the second machine age depends, wrote Reyner Banham, on the architect's willingness to unload his cultural swag in emulation of the Futurists and to divest himself of the 'professional garments by which he is recognized as an architect.'[74] From a distance, Frei Otto appears to personify Banham's description of a front runner with technology. None of the conventional professional garments fit Frei Otto, for he is an amalgam of architect, engineer and inventor. Frei Otto's detachment from aesthetic involvements, typified by his approach to form which springs from a knowledge of structure, casts his role within the mainstream of functionalism. The rational clarity of Newtonian physics supplies the essential ideas for his experimentation with lightweight construction. He believes that the efficient solution of the building task requires the optimal management of minimal material. Frei Otto is 'interested in a form with minimal material to develop out of the function . . .'[75]

This straightforward assessment of Frei Otto as a functionalist is belied by the persistent beauty of his structures and their observance of prominent third generation inflexions. The same German creative tradition which informed Mies' architecture pervades Frei Otto's form-making. Their patient search for architectural perfection is conditioned by a mental reflex which reduces reality to a few universal design problems and so allows them to strip it down to an ultimate minimal expression. Paul Rudolph's criticism of Mies applies with equal force to Frei Otto. Each makes 'wonderful buildings only because he ignores many aspects of building. If he solved more problems, his buildings would be far less potent'.[76]

The heavy incidence of third-generation commitments in Frei Otto's lightweight structures provides an unselfconscious confirmation of these values. He epitomizes a major third-generation drive, the urge towards a minimal structure, 'to accomplish a task with minimum use of materials is finally the only interesting problem'.[77] An overt futurism connects Frei Otto with the fantasy world of Archigram. The first generation's aesthetic of hovering forms, recaptured in Utzon's sketches, is most convincingly realized by Frei Otto's tension nets. The contrasting poetic images of light floating roofs suspended above heavy earth platforms is ideally expressed by the language of tension.

Frei Otto's conception of physical flexibility arises from his understanding of the behaviour of tension structures under variable loading conditions. Tension structures are inherently flexible. They assume a distinct topography for every loading

*Buildings and Projects*

Bandstand for the Federal Garden Exhibition, Kassel, 1955

Dance Pavilion, Federal Garden Exhibition, Cologne, 1957

Entrance Arch, Federal Garden Exhibition, Cologne, 1957

Open-air Theatre roof, Nijmegen, 1960–1

Dock Cover, Bremen, 1961

Open-air Theatre roof, Wunsiedel, 1962

Wave Hall, International Horticultural Exhibition, Hamburg, 1963

Small Pavilions, International Horticultural Exhibition, Hamburg, 1963

'Snow and Rocks' Pavilions, Swiss National Exhibition, Lausanne, 1964

Cologne Fair Umbrellas, 1964

Medical Academy at Ulm University, 1965

Federal German Pavilion, Expo '67, Montreal, 1965–7

Conference Centre and Hotel in Riyadh, Saudi Arabia, 1966

Open-air Theatre roof, Bad Hersfeld, 1968

Stadia roofs for the 1972 Olympic Games, Munich, 1968–72

Roofs for Sports Centre, Kuwait, 1969

Architect's own house, Stuttgart, 1970

Hoechst Stadium roof, Hanover, 1970

Olympic Stadium roof, Berlin, 1970

Entertainments Centre, Monte Carlo, Monaco, 1970

1. The bandstand shelter for the Federal Garden Exhibition at Kassel in Germany, 1955, was the first tent design by Frei Otto to be built. The four-point surface was stretched between two high and two low points.

condition because they lack bending stiffness. Frei Otto devised special clamps which allow individual cable strands in the tension net to move under changing loads. The natural flexibility of tension structures was amplified in his series of retractable umbrellas at the Cologne Fair (p. 125) and the adaptable roofs for open air theatres and stadia.

Frei Otto's interest in creating structures which adapt to changing patterns of human use is a logical extension of the essential flexibility found in tension structures. Aerospace technologies' investigation of multi-role performance in the sixties parallels the architectural phenomenon. Following on from Barnes Wallis' suggestions for a variable geometry craft, the General Dynamics Corporation produced the swing-wing FI-11 aircraft.

The ideal of a minimal architectural equipage, and pursuit of individual freedom in the environment was an important discovery shared by Frei Otto with Archigram and Kikutake. Archigram's nihilism and criticism of rigid systems of order for the environment accords with the solutions found by Frei Otto during the research at the Institute of Lightweight Structures at Stuttgart University. The building is serviced by a perimeter loop of hot-water pipes, with valves at close intervals to permit mobile work places to be plugged-in to the heating system wherever desired.

From his family, Frei Otto inherited a sensitivity to form which predisposed him towards a concrete definition of structural problems. The importance which modelling techniques assume as integrated design and analytical tools complements his intuitive approach which is backed by a fluent knowledge of physics. This essentially creative method is especially suited to indeterminate structural tasks which resist mathematical analysis.

A repertoire of three types: soap bubble, curtain material and structural models ensures a progressive involvement in the analysis of a structure. The significance of the soap bubble models is that they generate surfaces of minimum tension, which enable Frei Otto to establish a membrane topography with an equal tensile force per unit area. This in turn allows him to use the same weight of cable and a uniform net throughout the structure. In the second stage, small curtain material (polyester) models explain the real effect of the forms. The final structural models prove the stress in the nets and define the exact length of the cables. With the exception of the initial soap bubble models, the models serve as an analytical tool for evaluating the structural validity of a form.

2. The star-shaped membrane roof over the open-air Dance Pavilion at the Federal Garden Exhibition at Cologne in 1957 undulates in sympathy with the human context.

3. The dynamic sweep of the translucent membrane provided a dramatic introduction to the Garden Exhibition at Cologne and to Frei Otto's tent constructions.

4. A side view shows the cotton membrane supported on a low 34 m tubular steel arch.

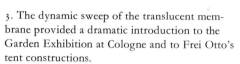

An example of the refinement of special aspects of a problem noted in the architecture of Mies van der Rohe is found in Frei Otto's systematic development of tension membranes. The early garden tent designs used pure membranes of PVC coated polyester fabric. The technical innovation of cable nets sewn into the canvas with plastic sleeves for the Swiss National Exhibition Pavilions at Lausanne (p. 119) represented a significant departure. The absence of shear in cable nets compared with membranes made it feasible to build at a greater scale. A noticeable behavioural discrepancy between the net and membrane at Lausanne caused Frei Otto to separate the two elements in the later Federal German Pavilion for Expo '67, Montreal (p. 120). There, the main plastic membrane was suspended about a foot below the steel cable net on hundreds of hangers, and attached by means of two foot diameter load-spreading quatrefoil rosettes. A membrane of standard plastic panels was lifted above the cable net for the 1972 Munich Olympic Games stadium roofs (pp. 122–3) by combined cable clamp and pedestal supports.

The early series of Frei Otto tents (Bandstand, Kassel, p. 115; Wave Hall, Hamburg, p. 118; and Dance Pavilion, Cologne, p. 115) improvized traditional themes with an incomparable sensitivity to the logic and aesthetic of tension. An unrivalled empathy was elicited between the flowing terrain of these elegant shelters and their landscape settings. Despite their imposing size and increasing sophistication, the Lausanne pavilions belong to this traditional tent vernacular. The technical solutions pioneered in the Montreal roofs raised the design of tents from the status of a craft tradition to a sophisticated engineering discipline, and greatly expanded their potential usefulness. By alternately propping up the cable net on eight steel masts and pulling it down in funnels, Frei Otto countered the effects of flutter. High stress concentrations at the mast supports were avoided by the expedient of eye-cables which gathered the stresses over a large area and looped back to the point of origin. The outline of the Montreal pavilion was conditioned by the shape of the site and the height required for the route through the pavilion. Exhibition areas were independently disposed beneath the roof on steel and timber chair-like platforms. The seemingly arbitrary location of the eight steel masts obeyed a sort of free-hand geometrical discipline. Remarkably, the pavilion cost only £4 ($10) per square foot including transport from West Germany.

In order to optimize tension, it is necessary to build on an ample scale. The visionary projection of the idea to cover Bremen Harbour (p. 121) and even entire cities was an attempt by Frei Otto to visualize the potential efficiency of this structural medium. Although the roofs for the 1972 Olympic Games at Munich (pp. 122–3) are less than megastructures, they do establish a new scale of operation which was only hinted at in the Montreal pavilion. The covering roof for the main stadium consists of an independent sequence of radial petals hung from cigar-shaped (to resist bending) tubular steel masts and restrained by a continuous cable arch on the inside.

At Munich, Frei Otto has used two types of weatherproof membrane, a PVC-coated polyester fabric suspended on hangers below the cable net similar to Montreal, and flexible transparent acrylglas (plexiglass) panels supported on thumb-like pedestals. The study of tension structures (1950–3) led Frei Otto quite naturally to an exploration (1958–61) of the untouched potential of pneumatic structures. Air pressure substitutes for compression masts as the essential structural element for providing the equal and opposite force recognized by Newton's first law—'to every action there is an equal and opposite reaction'. He published his treatise on pneumatics, *Zugbeanspruchte Konstruktionen*, Vol. 1, prior to their adoption as a plaything of the architectural *avant-garde*. His injunction 'not (to) use them as novelties but wherever they can be an essential help in the solution of a particular task'[78] passed unheeded (1961). The *avant-garde's* failure to take pneumatics seriously, and its superficial equation of the principle with freedom on the basis of aesthetic novelty obscured the practical utility and real limitations of the new structural medium. The experimental application of air support to the solution of new problems offered an imaginative expansion of the idea, centred on the visual implications of pneumatic shapes. His troop of examples included: floating planting fields, underwater storage tanks, floating vehicular tunnels, gas and liquid containers, pillow structures (on the buttoned cushion or rubber air-bed theme), and superbubbles to contain harbours, reservoirs or cities.

The breadth of Frei Otto's structural interests ranges beyond the boundaries of tension. He used pure compression domes developed from hanging chain nets for the auditoria in the Federal German Pavilion, Montreal, and a similar solution was suggested for the Monaco scheme's compression roof. The triple humps which shade the Kuwait Sports Centre (p. 124) (architect: Kenzo Tange) were supported from compression arches in lieu of the usual masts.

His refusal to tickle the form of a structure to achieve an architectural effect is a measure of Frei Otto's dedication to producing new forms which have great structural purity, that is, direct force structures. The first generation's assumptions of rationalism and idealization, of simplicity over complexity and richness girds Frei Otto's structural decisions. Nevertheless, he stands as the third generation's most gifted and creative exponent of the structural approach to architectural form.

5

a

b

c

d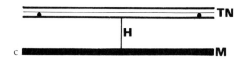

e

5. The systematic development and flexibility of Frei Otto's thought is revealed in his refinement of the roof details. Key: M membrane, TN tension net, H hanger, P pedestal support.
a. Pure membrane for small-scale garden tents.
b. The membrane reinforced by a tension net sewn into the canvas with plastic sleeves. Example: Swiss National Exhibiton Pavilions at Lausanne, 1964.
c. Membrane hung from the tension net for large structures. Example: Federal German Pavilion, Montreal, 1967.
d. Translucent roof panels supported off the tension net. The 1972 Olympic Games roofs employ this method and also the earlier detail.
e. A future synthesis of the tension net and membrane functions.

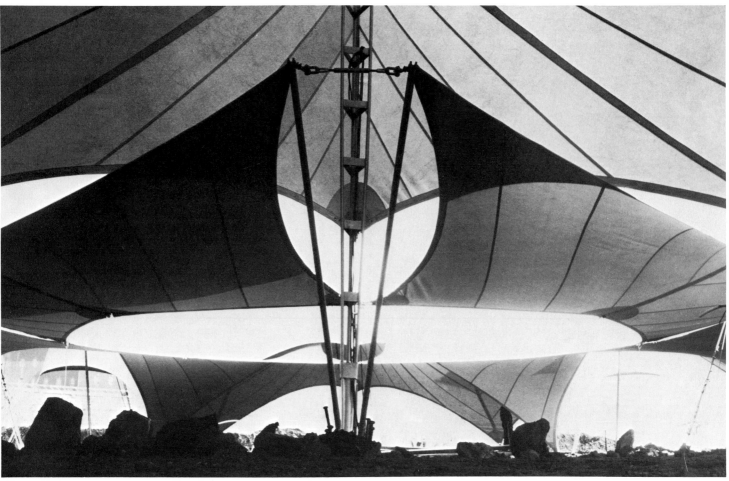

6

6. A cluster of four tent pavilions at the 1963 International Horticultural Exhibition in Hamburg were linked by an annular gallery.

7. Above the large unobstructed space at Hamburg in 1963, this sculptural undulating wave-shaped membrane easily conveys the potential of these structures.

8. A side view of one of the group of four peaked tents at the International Horticultural Exhibition in Hamburg. The star-shaped undulating configuration consisted of four high and four low points.

7

8

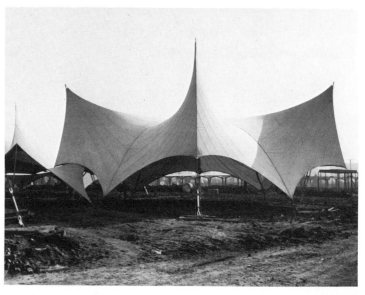

9

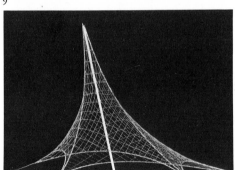

9. A group of five large interlocking white, yellow, and red tents marked the 'Snow and Rocks' section of the Swiss National Exhibition at Lausanne in 1964.

10. A preliminary study of the surfaces generated by one high and four low points.

11. The main loads were taken on the steel cable network, the membrane merely serving as a weatherproof enclosure.

12. The design for an exhibition building at Cologne, 1956–7, embodied the first proposal for a roof comprising alternate high and low points.

10

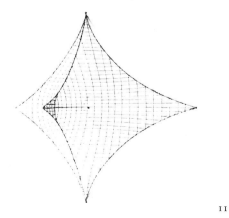

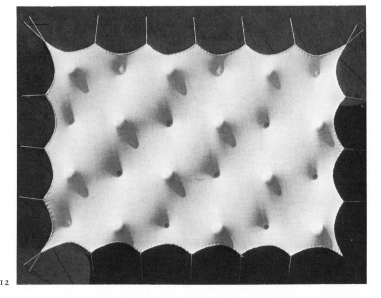

11              12

13

13. The roof scape of the Federal German Pavilion at Expo '67, Montreal, illuminated at night.
14. The impact of light steel cable nets, first effectively realized in the Montreal roof, bypassed traditional aesthetic categories and approached the first generation's ambition to construct floating transparent roof enclosures.

15. By alternately propping up the cable net on eight steel masts and pulling it down in funnels, Frei Otto countered the effects of flutter. The exhibition areas were disposed freely beneath the roof on modular steel and timber platform elements.

14

15

16, 17. The second scheme for a Medical Academy at Ulm University, 1965.
16. Side view of the fabric model.
17. Plan, view.

16

17

18. The visionary projection of the tension idea for a roof covering Bremen harbour, 1961, and later realized in the Munich Games roofs was an attempt to exploit the principle's inherent advantages for large span enclosures.

18

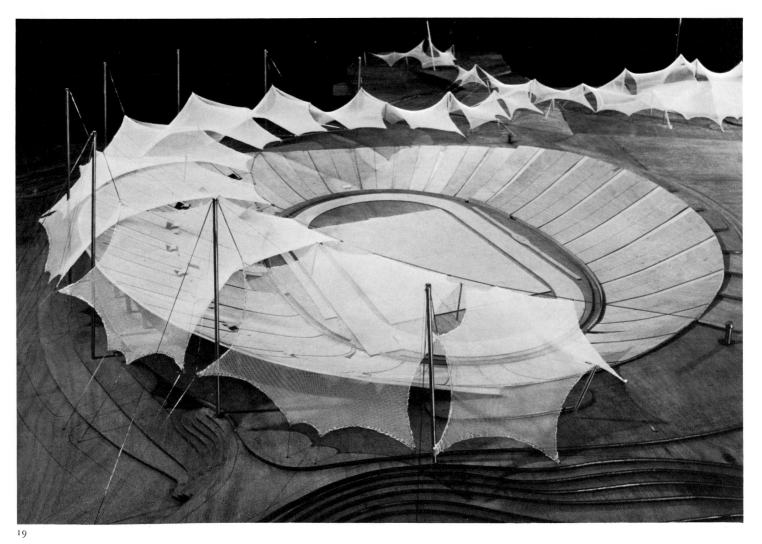

19

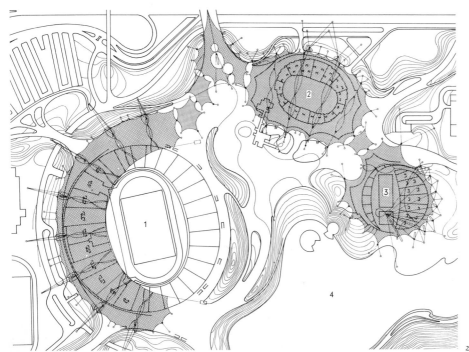

19–23. Roofs for the 1972 Olympic Games at Munich. Architects: Frei Otto with Behnisch & Partners.

19. A series of roof elements connect the main stadium with the athletic and swimming areas to the right.

20. Plan of the Olympic athletic facilities. Key: 1 stadium, 2 arena, 3 swimming area, 4 lake.

21. The weather covering of translucent sky reflecting acrylic glass panels sealed with neoprene profiles creates a roof topography akin to a well-eroded landscape.

22. Double exposure of part of the stadium net model. The distance between the white spots on the two exposures of the loaded and unloaded conditions show deformations due to loading.

23. Structural model test for the stand roof of the main Olympic Stadium. In order to avoid creep in the model, all photography was completed in the shortest practicable time using stereoscopic cameras to photograph deflections and strains before and after loading.

20

21

22

23

24

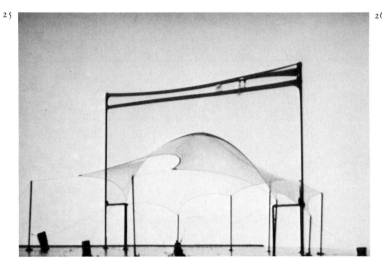

25

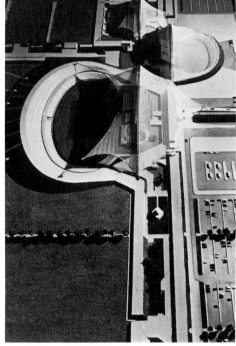

26

27

24–26. Kuwait Stadium roofs. Architects: Frei
Otto with Kenzo Tange and Urtec, 1969.
24. The sports centre was provided with three
individual roofs similar in concept to the Cologne
entrance roof.
25. Soap bubble model for the Kuwait stadium
competition.
26. The sports centre was to consist of three
stadia: a main stadium, an indoor arena and the
swimming pool, in effect a small olympic games
complex.

27. Olympic Stadium roof, Berlin. Competition
project, with Ove Arup Engineers, 1970.
The solution envisages a heavy weight roof
spanning between two large derricks cantilevered
from behind the stadium.

28

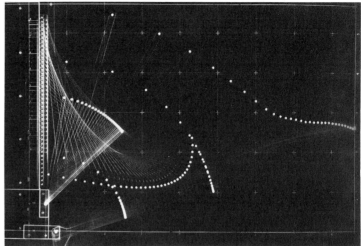

29

30

31

28–31. Cologne Fair umbrellas, 1964.
28. A multiple exposure photograph showing the mechanism for opening and closing the membrane which is very similar to an ordinary umbrella.
29. A multiple exposure photograph which traces the movement profiles of the movable strut supports.
30. Retractable roof mushroom in partially opened condition.
31. Umbrellas in fully extended profile.

32

32. Model study of a furlable peaked tent, 1962, for temporary protection against rain or sun.

33. Open-air Theatre, Bad Hersfeld, Germany, 1968.
The multiple exposure photograph shows the bunched membrane being unfurled over the ruins of the medieval church in preparation for a theatrical performance.

34–38. Open-air Theatre at Nijmegen, Holland, 1960–1.
34–37. Plan views of model at intermediate stages of unfurling.
38. Front view.

33

34

35

36

37

38

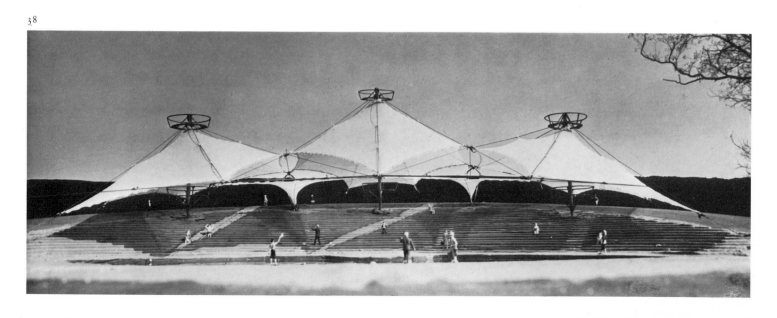

39

40

41

39, 40. Hoechst Stadium, Hanover, 1970.
39. A multiple exposure photograph of the model roof unfurling.
40. Brunched roof membrane suspended from pulleys on an offset mast.

41. Retractable roof for a concert arena, Wunsiedel, Germany, 1962.
Roof fully extended for a performance.

42

42. Pneumatic structures with low points, model, 1959. The visual similarity of pneumatic structures and biological skins maintained by hydrostatic pressure is evident.

43. Photomontage of a giant greenhouse consisting of a pneumatic envelope with low points protecting an orchard in a frigid climate, 1959.

44. Pneumatic model study for a festival hall set on a rectangular superstructure.

43

44

# James Stirling

The tough industrial vernacular of the Liverpool of his youth has placed a heavy accent on Stirling's architecture. He started life (1926) in Glasgow, but after four years the family moved to Liverpool. In pop mythology it is still a matter of conjecture whether the beatle John Lennon's attendance at Quarry Bank High School was influenced by the precedent of James Stirling. He settled down to studying architecture at Liverpool University (1945–50) after a quick dash across to the Normandy beaches on D-Day with the Black Watch. Through his teacher and intellectual mentor, Colin Rowe, who had been an outstanding pupil of Rudolf Wittkower, Stirling acquired an insight into the classical foundations of modern architecture which surfaced in some of his later works.

Stirling and James Gowan left Lyons, Israel and Ellis where they had been senior assistants and set up in partnership on the strength of the Ham Common commission. The recommendation of Sir Leslie Martin led to the Leicester University Engineering Building scheme (pp. 136–7), which established their international reputation and saved the embryonic firm from dissolution. The increasing recognition of the value of Stirling's architecture outside England attracted numerous lecturing engagements, culminating in the Museum of Modern Art's *Three Buildings of James Stirling* exhibition in 1968. Stirling's pursuit of purely architectural results outside the mainstream of commercial architecture assures his designs of continuing significance.

Le Corbusier's abandonment in the fifties of the rational ideology he helped inspire precipitated the crisis of rationalism in the modern movement. Unlike Utzon who found himself in sympathy with Le Corbusier's new outlook, James Stirling became convinced that the heavy concrete and primitive folk ancestry of Le Corbusier's forms was alien to 'the spirit of modern architecture'. In an article on the Maisons Jaoul which appeared in the *Architectural Review* (September 1955), Stirling voiced his unease: 'It is disturbing to find little reference to *the rational principles which are the basis of the modern movement*'.[79] (author's italics) Recently, he acknowledged 'much as I am an admirer of Corbusier . . . *I've always regretted that last period of Corbusier's work*'.[80] (author's italics)

Not far from the Ham Common Flats (pp. 132–3), a design which consummated Stirling's allegiance to Le Corbusier's new mode, Burton's Palm House in Kew Gardens (p. 131) proffered an escape from the impasse of an embattled rationalism. The architecture of James Stirling is a passion play re-enacting the genesis of modern architecture. After Ham Common, Stirling embarked on a heroic and lonely journey commencing with the gestation of modern architecture in the second decade of the twentieth century. In his replay of modern architecture, he fended off the dangerously irrelevant stylistic detour of the Cubist machine aesthetic by resorting to the nineteenth-century engineering vernacular with which England is richly endowed.

The association of James Stirling with Brutalism instigated by Reyner Banham raised anti-aesthetic expectations which were not supported by his architecture. Stirling wisely dissociated himself from Brutalism. He told Arata Isozaki that there was in England 'a feeling of national guilt about architecture . . ., that making a building is somehow sinful or that spending so much money is somehow evil . . . I don't contribute to this'.[81] The subjection of English architecture to the sentimental and moral exercises of a powerful literary tradition inhibited the emergence of a purely plastic sensibility. In the post-Renaissance history of English Architecture, few really creative figures managed to exceed the limiting values of the prevailing literary

*Buildings and Projects*

Sheffield University Competition, 1953
Village Project (C.I.A.M.10), 1955
Flats at Ham Common, Richmond, 1956–8
Infill-Housing at Preston, Lancashire, 1958–60
Selwyn College extension, Project, 1959
Engineering Building, Leicester University, 1959–63
History Faculty Building, Cambridge University, 1964–7
Andrew Melville Hall, St. Andrews, 1964–8
Dorman Long Project, 1965
Queen's College New Residence, Oxford, 1967–71
Low-cost Housing Project for Lima, Peru, 1969
Olivetti Training Centre, Haslemere, 1969
New Computer Centre, Siemens A.G., Munich, 1970

culture and assert an abstract architectural vision. Thus, although Stirling exorcized the sentimental and picturesque from his work, preferring instead the simple geometric forms of the nineteenth-century engineering vernacular, his attitude could hardly be construed as anti-aesthetic, or Brutalist. At the most, it was anti-literati. He believes that 'the quality of an environment is almost entirely the result of making the correct three-dimensional physical proposals'.[82] Possibly the experience of aesthetic censorship exercised by incompetent planners which deprived him of four out of six house commissions when he was starting out in private practice intensified his mistrust of supra-architectural pretensions.

James Stirling's pursuit of a regional vernacular architecture adjusted to specific contexts was encouraged by the postwar regionalism of Le Corbusier. Participation in the independent group (1954–6) strengthened Stirling's enthusiasm for popular culture and directed his energy towards the creation of a contemporary vernacular in tune with popular consciousness. His architecture explored two specifically English fields: the brick domestic tradition and the nineteenth-century cast-iron and glass engineering aesthetic. Because he is deeply conscious of the historical traditions of his profession, Stirling's reconstruction of select English vernaculars is overlaid by sophisticated reiterations of concepts peculiar to the early period of modern architecture.

In a project for C.I.A.M.10 in 1955, Stirling devised an extensible linear system for rural housing based on the traditional English village. Another scheme developed an idea from the backs of terrace housing. The Ham Common Flats (pp. 132–3) and Infill-Housing at Preston, Lancashire (pp. 134–5), were sophisticated permutations of this brick vernacular leavened with sculptural intimations of the Maisons Jaoul and De Stijl aesthetics. Stirling justified his appropriation of glass building in terms of the English climate: 'Glass buildings are, I think, appropriate in the English climate. We are perhaps the only country where it is seldom too hot or too cold, and on a normal cloudy day, there is a high quality of diffused light in the sky. A glass covering keeps the rain out and lets the light through.'[83]

Glass architecture belonged to the first-generation catechism and Stirling's revival of that futuristic vision as the authentic image of functionalism extended researches commenced in 1914 by Paul Scheerbart and Bruno Taut. James Stirling enveloped the reading area of the Cambridge History Faculty Building (pp. 138–9) with a stepped pyramid consisting of a double glazed skin separated by an air space containing lighting, structure and ventilation exhausts. Scheerbart had described a similar arrangement in *Glas Architektur* half a century before Stirling implemented it with such spectacular effect. The likelihood that Stirling was unaware of Scheerbart's proposal recommends the view that the adoption of identical objectives tends to produce similar conclusions. The Selwyn College project which followed Stirling's visit to the Pierre Chareau Glass House in Paris (1958) was the first of a series of such projects which included the Leicester (pp. 136–7), Cambridge (pp. 138–9), Oxford (p. 142) and Dorman Long (p. 141) buildings.

Daunted by very low cost and profitability, their former employees—Lyons, Israel and Ellis—generously offered Stirling and Gowan the Preston slum clearance project. They showed their gratitude by converting it into a Ministry of Housing Award for Good Design. Much of Stirling's early housing work was undertaken under conditions of extreme economic austerity. The savings accrued from the selection of standard inexpensive materials such as brick and patent glazing were invested in raising the architectural quality of the environment. Stirling and Gowan's ability to extract maximum design opportunity in the most unpropitious circumstances demonstrates a rare combination of pragmatic realism and design imagination.

1. Palm House, Kew Gardens. Designer: Decimus Burton, 1844.
Nineteenth-century engineering iron and glass vernacular.

I

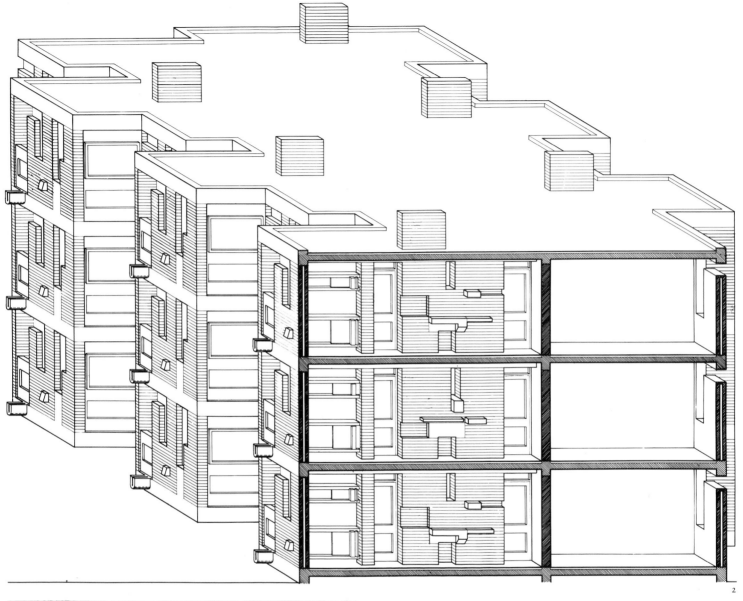

2

3

2–7. Flats at Ham Common, Richmond. Architects: James Stirling and James Gowan, 1956–8.
2. Section through three-storey block. The forceful modelling of brick and concrete in the rough comes off as mildly Brutalist.
3. Rear elevation facing park.
4. Aerial view of the narrow Ham Common site.
5. Plan, upper floor of two-storey block.
6. A first floor bridge connects all three flats with the stair and opens up the circulation common.
7. Stair, exterior.

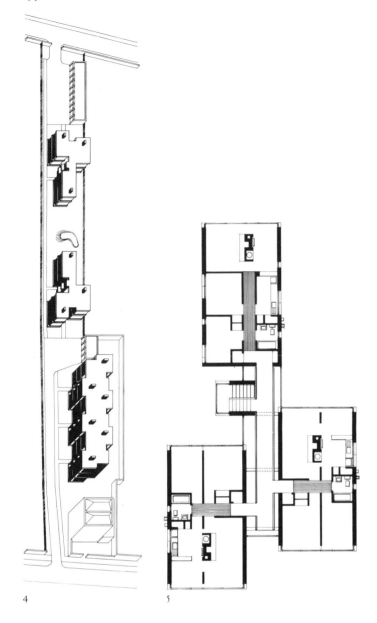

4

5

6

7

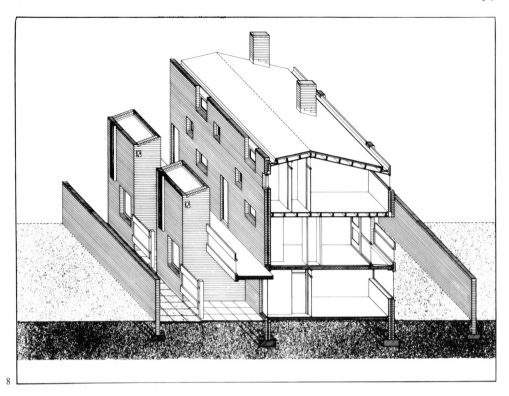

8–10. Infill-Housing at Preston, Lancashire. Architects: James Stirling and James Gowan, 1958–60.
8. Axonometric section.
9. View of street façade, north block.
10. Site.

8

The set-back tapered profile of the Chrysler building type of New York skyscraper provides 'a graphic expression of metropolitan pressure' which exemplifies a recurrent theme in Stirling's architecture. The topography of the Leicester University building's overall form and the reducing section of the main stair-tower are examples of this. According to the gravitational principle which informed the Cambridge, Oxford and Dorman Long projects, spaces tend to establish their level in the vertical hierarchy according to size and public accessibility. All three buildings were set on brick podia or platforms—which agrees with Giedion's characterization of the third-generation principle.

The Brutalist label, applied to Stirling, conjures up broad expanses of coarse board marked off-form concrete. Stirling derides heavy concrete as an 'Egyptian' method of construction, and in practice he rarely exposes his concrete because '. . . I began to question the whole idea of using concrete as a modern building method'. He prefers to clad his buildings in neat red engineering brick and matching Dutch tiles, a far cry from *béton brut*. Furthermore, the superior weathering of these materials is a real asset in the English climate.

In the fashion of a Karate wrestler, Stirling gains additional leverage from the realities of the situation. The brief for the Leicester University Engineering Building required a north-light workshop and one hundred feet hydraulic supply to be provided on a tight unsuitably orientated site. These realities imposed the forty-five degree roof geometry on the structural grid, and raised the slender office tower to support a water tank. Stirling uses restrictions as thrust blocks to launch a design. The layout of the Faculty of History Building was predicated on the provision of unobstructed sight-lines from the control desk over the reading and stack areas, controlled access and excellent natural lighting. Andrew Melville Hall at St. Andrews University (p. 140) re-used the superimposed dual geometries developed for Leicester under the guise of ensuring favourable views of the Scottish landscape from the individual student cells.

Sir Leslie Martin exercised a decisive influence on Stirling through his representa-

9

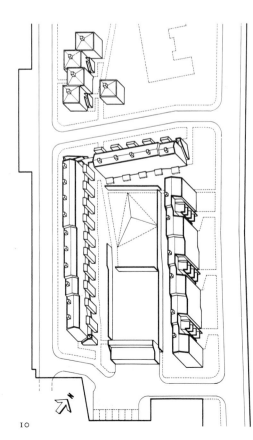

10

tion of the theory of endless architecture. The concept of buildings as endlessly repetitive linear extensions derived in the early fifties from a simplified interpretation of the significance of mass production. It called into existence an aesthetic whose point was visual repetition. The repetition of standard elements is enshrined as a universal reality of technological society in Stirling's work. It effects his selection of standard materials and articulation of structure, space and circulation in terms of standard modules. The mechanical assembly of rooms along a horizontal circulation spine or 'driving axle' made its debut in Stirling's Sheffield University competition entry of 1953. He extended the concept to the Dorman Long (p. 141) and Siemens (p. 143) schemes, which are extreme projections of endless architecture.

Stirling meticulously observes the first generation injunction to articulate separate functions. Different materials and plastic elements were separated in the two-storey flat units at Ham Common. The sculptural complexity of the Leicester University Engineering Building derived in part from Stirling's insistence that each form express a single function. The relative intensity and juxtaposition of different internal functions is scrupulously recorded in the sculptural modelling of the external building envelope. Stirling's obsession with single functional categories ignores the third-generation's distaste for simple hierarchical and functional structures which avoid ambiguity and overlap.

The Dorman Long and Siemens projects reveal the emergence of a classicizing trend in Stirling's designs, allied to a superhuman technological repertoire of forms. The total image of both projects is thoroughly mechanical. The architectural character evoked by the pedestrian Mall which bisects the Siemens A.G. computer centre is a tank farm transplanted from Cape Kennedy, a type of heavy Berlin Neo-classicism.

James Stirling's architecture attains a reformative significance through the protestant quality of his vision of modern architecture which inspired him to rework the first generation lode. The uncompromising strength and purity of his forms rank with the best in English architecture.

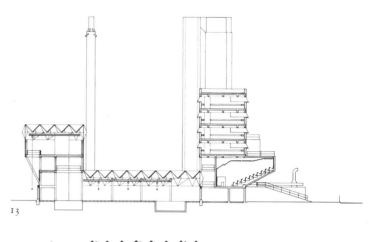

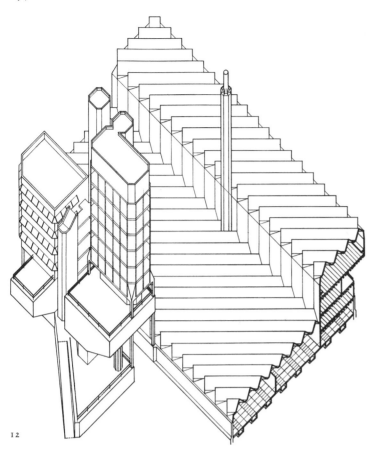

11–16. Engineering Building, Leicester University. Architects: James Stirling and James Gowan, 1959–63.

11. View.

12. Axonometric of the building from the southwest.

13. Section through main lecture theatre.

14. Plan, first floor.

15. Section, glazed workshop roof.

16. Night view of circulation core.

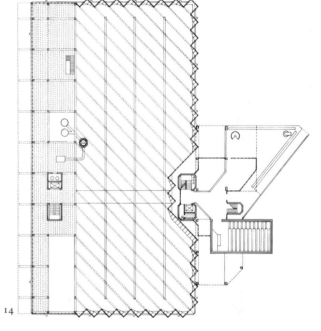

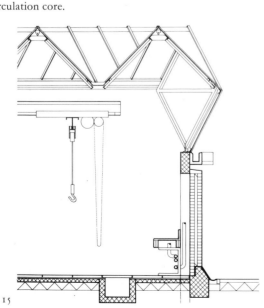

17

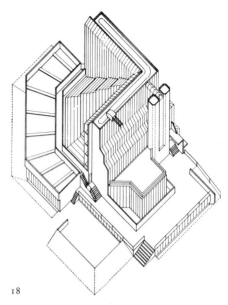

18

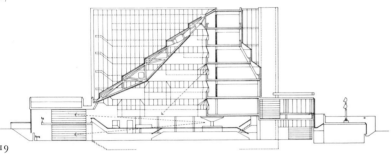

19

20

17–23. History Faculty Building, Cambridge University, 1964–7.
17. East elevation.
18. Axonometric.
19. North-south section through the main reading room.

20. Air extract equipment and steel structure silhouetted against the underside of the glass roof.
21. Plan, first floor.
22. Plan, fourth floor.
23. Main reading room.

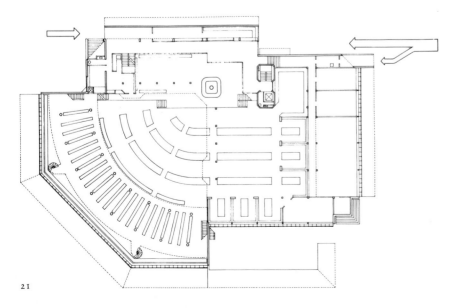

21

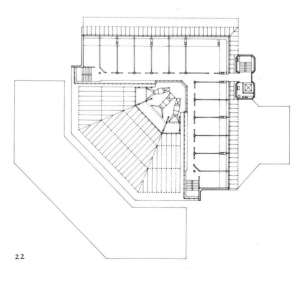

22

24

25

26

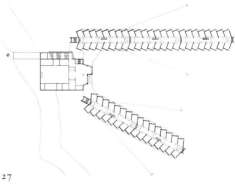

27

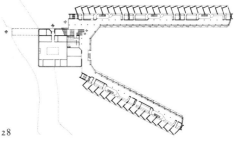

28

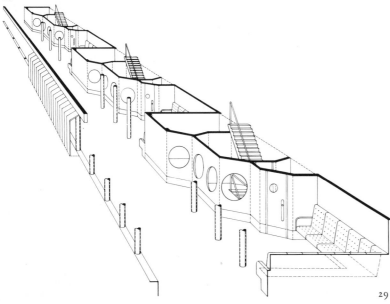

29

24–29. Andrew Melville Hall, St. Andrews, 1964–8.

24. First hall of residence.

25. The site overlooks St. Andrews bay set against the Scottish mountains.

26. Diagonal ribbed precast concrete wall elements facing the student study-bedrooms with the fully glazed promenade.

27. Plan at typical level.

28. Plan at level of the promenade gallery.

29. Cut-away axonometric shows social alcoves feeding off the circulation promenade.

30

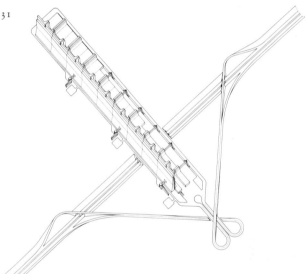

31

30–33. Dorman Long Project, 1965.
30. View of model.
31. Axonometric of three stage development
approaches the condition of endless architecture.
Uneven extrusion of a typical building section.
32. Canted glazed wall section.
33. Model showing structure outside the glass
skin and diagonal wired bracing.

32

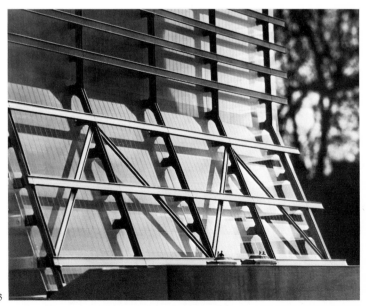

33

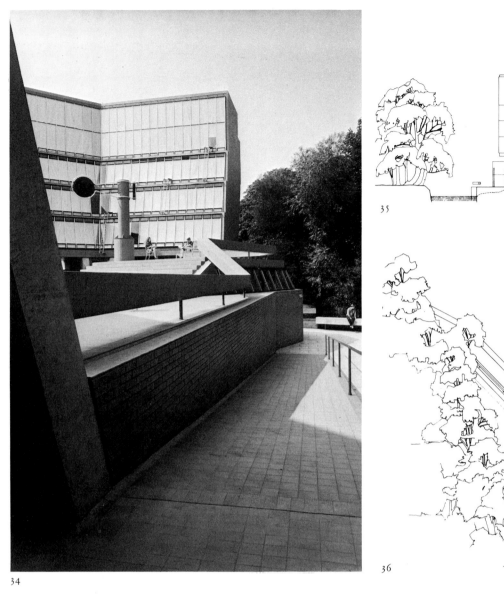

34

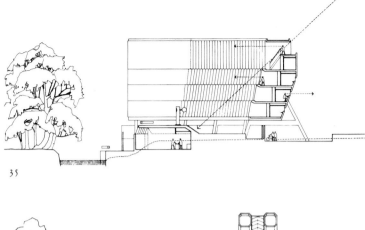

35

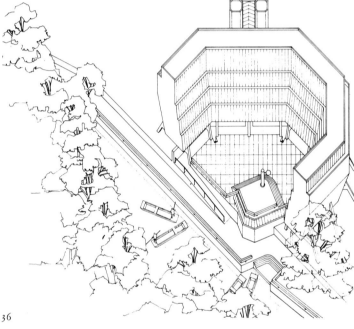

36

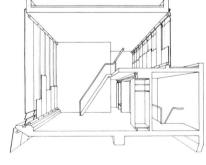

37

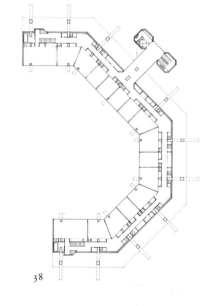

38

34–38. Queen s College, New Residence, Oxford, 1967–71.

34. View of horse-shoe-shaped college deck from river side.

35. Section.

36. Axonometric.

37. Section, typical and study-bedroom.

38. Plan, first floor.

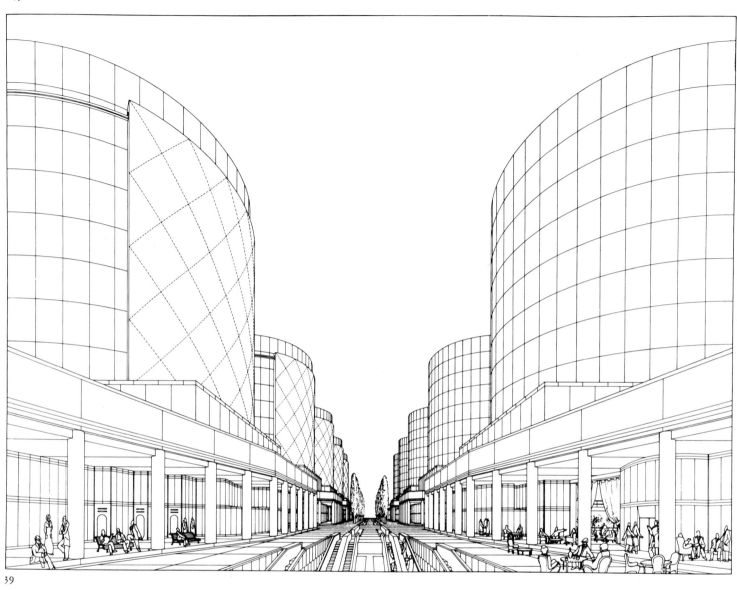

39

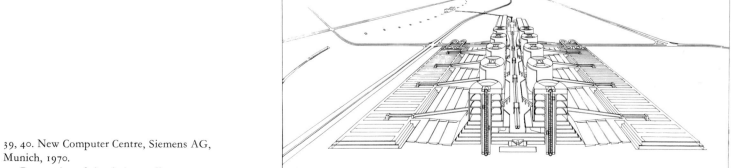

39, 40. New Computer Centre, Siemens AG,
Munich, 1970.
39. Perspective of circulation wall.
40. Axonometric, total development.

40

# John Andrews

John Andrews was born in Sydney, Australia (1933) and studied architecture at Sydney University (1956). While completing his masters degree at Harvard, he and some fellow students submitted an entry in the international competition for the design of the new Toronto City Hall and Office complex. Andrews' submission, which was placed second, brought him to the attention of J. B. Parkin and the competition victor, the distinguished Finnish architect, Viljo Revell, who was so impressed by Andrews' ability after a nine-month association that he funded Andrews' world study tour (1961–2). Andrews returned to Canada, more by accident than design, and set up a private practice subsisting on kitchen renovations. Part-time teaching at the University of Toronto led to his involvement in the planning of a satellite college. Seizing the moment, Andrews finalized the design of Scarborough College in a galloping six weeks, and construction was completed in the remarkably short space of two years. An article in *Time* Magazine put Andrews on the world's news-stands. In 1967, John Andrews was appointed chairman of the architectural department of the University of Toronto as a full-time professor and initiated a new curriculum. The Andrews practice is international in scope and seeks to optimize individual talent through co-operative design focused on creative problem-solving.

At the very moment when English Brutalism was losing its nerve, John Andrews touched down with one of the most brutally frank buildings of the decade. Scarborough College (pp. 146–7) embodied a number of Brutalist ideals—a rude expression of materials and the assembly of learning laboratories along an internal pedestrian street. John Andrews is a Brutalist by temperament rather than by commitment. Whereas English Brutalism was typically intellectual and sought its justification in an ethic, John Andrews' tough-minded functionalism is instinctive.

The creative force of Scarborough College arises from an original interpretation of an existing repertoire, carried forward with immense conviction and decisiveness. Much of the aesthetic inconsistency and brutal power of Scarborough resides in the architect's refusal to dissemble function for the sake of art. At the University of Guelph Student residences (p. 148), the separate articulation of the horizontal pedestrian circulation grid from the vertical student towers and the visual dissonance which has resulted was accepted as a candid reflection of necessity.

Indeed, John Andrews' approach might be summarized as architectural realism. The acceptance of complexity and contradiction possesses a theoretical nicety almost wholly absent in practice, and the first field casualty to a strategy which genuinely accepts the realities of the situation is art. It requires a determined and clear-headed acceptance of reality to forego the seductive ambulations of art. Scarborough College (pp. 146–7), the Guelph Student Residences (p. 148), the Miami Terminal (p. 149), Belconnen Government offices (p. 149) and the Harvard Graduate School of Design (p. 150) testify to the persistence of John Andrews' alliance with reality. The rich complexity of Scarborough College tends to obscure the forthright clarity of the founding concepts; linear growth along a circulation spine, organization by section, and topography. With a sharp eye for terrain, John Andrews modelled the building astride the plateau escarpment which commands a deeply-etched ravine to the south. This strategy permitted the pedestrian streets to be located at an intermediate level, with access directly on to the plateau floor, and eliminated the necessity for elevators. The organic alignment of the streets, accessibility, generous scale and weatherprofness ensured a social viability far in advance of the Golden Lane (1952) and Park Hill (1961) essays. John Andrews has since mobilized the pedestrian

*Buildings and Projects*

Belmere Public School, Scarborough, Ontario, 1964–5
Scarborough College, phase 1, Scarborough, Ontario, 1964–7
Student Housing Complex 'B', University of Guelph, Ontario, 1965
Steel plug-in Apartment Tower, 1965
African Place for Expo '67, Montreal, 1965
Activity Area 'F', Expo '67, Montreal, 1965
Commonwealth Place, Expo '67, Montreal, 1965
Weldon Library, London, Ontario, 1967
Metro Centre, Toronto, 1967
Student Centre, Toronto, 1967
Miami Passenger Terminal, Miami Beach, Florida, 1967
Library, Sarah Lawrence College, 1968
Belconnen Government office complex, Canberra, 1968
Art Building, Smith College, 1968
Graduate School of Design, Harvard University, 1969

1, 2. African Place, Expo '67, Montreal, 1965.
1. View at night from canal.
2. Axonometric view of village complex clustered around a central community plaza.

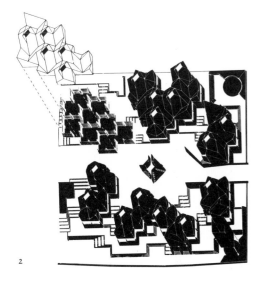

2

street in the Guelph Student Housing and the Belconnen Government offices.

At the crossroads of the science and humanities wings, Andrews threw up a monumental sky-lit meeting place to serve as a social focus for the college community numbering six thousand students. The persistent reiteration of the street and meeting-place ideas is evidence of a determination to foster spontaneous social interaction as an accompaniment of circulation. Andrews' observation that 'in these terms (informal learning), *communication is circulation:* how and when people move, origins and destinations, the variety of experiences along the way, the ability to extend the range of experiences' (author's italics) parallels Kurokawa's description of infrastructuring. Coincidentally, John Andrews' design practice elucidates Kurokawa's distinction between fibre form and porous space. Scarborough College is a brilliant exposition of fibre form, and the rationale for Guelph and Sarah Lawrence College demonstrates the universal logic of Kurokawa's notation of porous space. In both instances, the form develops from the multiplication of typical cell clusters consisting of nodes made up of three or six square spatial cells.

Much of the architectural drama of Scarborough accrued from Andrews' clever manipulation of the staggered section, a device which he returned to at Belconnen and the Harvard Graduate School of Design. The prestige of the Harvard commission and its close proximity to Le Corbusier's Carpenter Center just two blocks east of the G.S.D. site, elicited the most significant design to come from Andrews' office since Scarborough. Even though the client smothered much of the educational radicalism contained in the original submission, the approved scheme preserves the essential physical dispositions. The spatial openness and interconnection of the design studios was justified as a source of informal interaction between students and staff. The scheme consists of an inclined tray of overlapping studios covered by a great trussed roof of tubular steel. On the underside a lecture theatre, library and exhibition space face onto a sheltered pedestrian concourse.

The Graduate School of Design introduces a smooth international performer, whose sophisticated good looks, tailored in East Coast Modern, hardly suggests the rough honesty which was such an attractive quality in John Andrews' early work. It is an Australian vanity to believe that direct forthrightness is preferable to civilized deceit, and to a remarkable degree, John Andrews' early work, by its rude honesty, reflected a genuine architecture of complexity and contradiction.

3

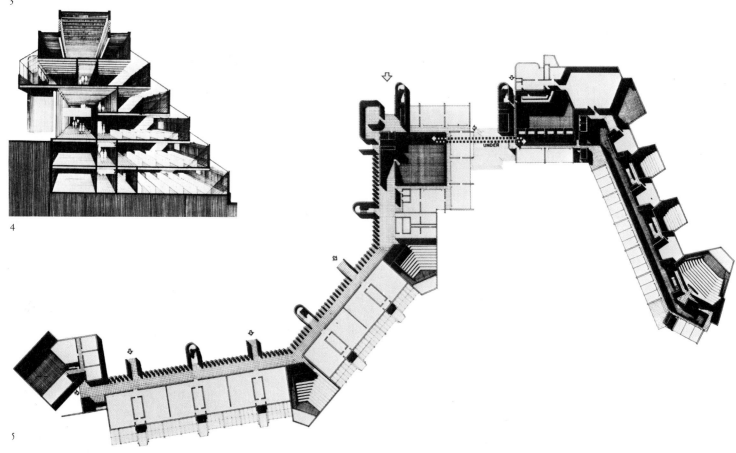

4

5

3–8. Scarborough College, phase 1, Scarborough, Ontario, 1964–7.

3. Aerial view in winter. The building follows the line of the plateau escarpment which falls steeply into a wooded ravine.

4. Section through laboratory floors, west wing.

5. Plan, pedestrian circulation street at plateau level.

6. A gap between the Science and Humanities wings breaks the continuity of the articulated building trunk and provides a visual link with the ravine which falls away to the south.

7. Section through the monumental sky-lit meeting place which serves as a social focus for the large college community.

8. The lecture blocks attached to the east face of the Humanities wing recall the expressive forms of unselfconscious architecture.

6

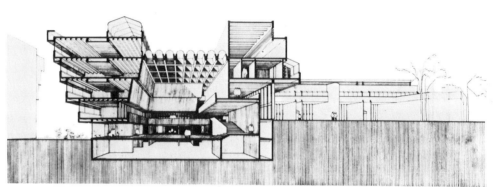

7

8

9

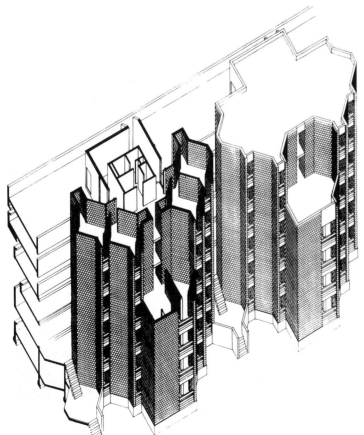

9–11. Student Housing Complex 'B', Guelph University, Ontario, 1965.
9. Aerial view.
10. Axonometric. The separate articulation of the horizontal pedestrian grid from the vertical student towers results in a wild case of architectural schizophrenia.
11. Plan, at pedestrian street level.

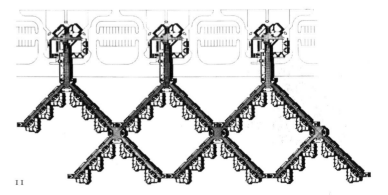

10

11

12, 13. Miami Passenger Terminal, Miami Beach, Florida, 1967.
12. View of passenger processing nodes from the waterfront.
13. Aerial view. The anti-architecture aesthetic of endless architecture explored by James Stirling in his Dorman Long project was convincingly realized at Miami.

12

13

14–16. Belconnen Government office complex, Canberra. Project, 1968.
14. View of the eastern connecting bridge which links the office fingers.
15. Aerial view of model from the west.
16. Section through model. The structural system consists of standard precast concrete floor and column elements.

15

14

16

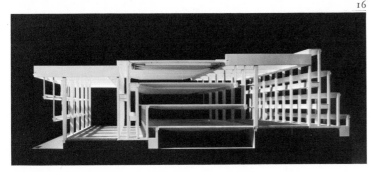

17

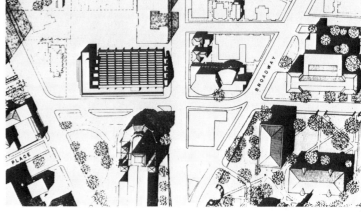

18

17–20. Graduate School of Design, Harvard
University, 1969.
17. View of model from south-west.
18. Site plan. The building is located two blocks
east of Le Corbusier's Carpenter Center.
19. View of model interior. The spatial openness
and interconnection of the design studios was
justified as a source of informal interaction between students and staff.
20. Section.

19

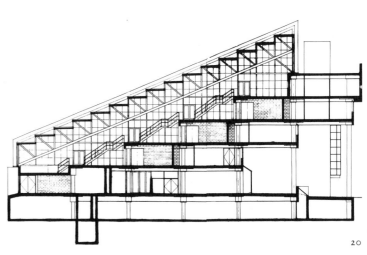

20

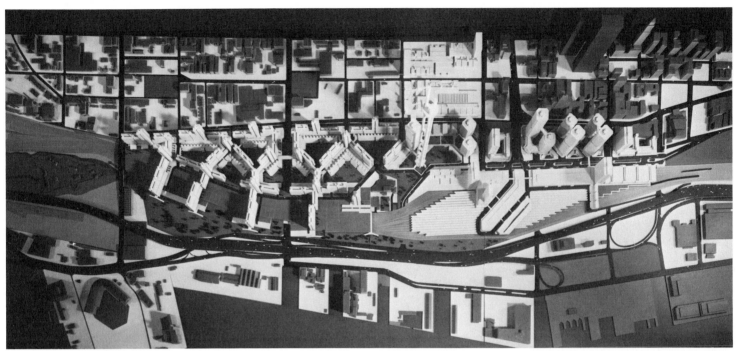

21

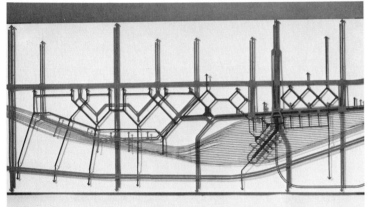

22

21–23. Metro Centre, Toronto, Ontario. Project, 1967.
21. Aerial view of model.
22. A Canada-wide railway network knots together along the Toronto waterfront and the complexity of the vehicular, rail and pedestrian circulation nets demanded an intensive analysis of the traffic systems.
23. View of the model from the east.

23

## Venturi and Rauch

Venturi and Rauch is a partnership which corrals the design initiatives of Denise Scott-Brown and Gerod Clark with those of the two principals. They are a strong group of individuals who share enthusiasms and an antipathy for 'heroic and original' architecture. Robert Venturi was born in Philadelphia in 1925, and graduated from Princeton (1950). He worked in the offices of Saarinen and Kahn (1956), whom he met while completing the Rome Prize. Since 1963 Venturi has taught at Yale University where he is the Charlotte Shepherd Davenport Professor of Architecture. Venturi's deep sense of history, and involvement with pop culture were combined in his design testament *Complexity and Contradiction in Architecture*, published by the Museum of Modern Art in 1966. John Rauch brings to the partnership (1964) a sensitive analytical mind and a wide knowledge of construction and costs. For twelve years, Venturi's close collaborator, Denise Scott-Brown, has supplied the social basis and pop insights into the group's architectural argument.

A number of third-generation architects, including Robert Venturi, sought an anonymous pattern vocabulary refined from available vernacular landscapes. The value of a pattern catalyst is to dramatize and differentiate the pattern product, usually a building, from the pattern resource. Third-generation architects favoured Expressionism or Futurism as the most effective pattern catalysts for liberating patterns from vernacular landscapes. In the absence of a powerful expressionism, James Stirling's recital of the English industrial vernacular would be almost indistinguishable from the pattern source.

Robert Venturi deferred the use of Expressionism or Futurism, and chose instead an extremely mild and subtle pattern catalyst, identified as Mannerism. He varied the intensity of his mannerist projection of the American commercial vernacular, and its primary manifestation the commercial strip, according to a flexible formula governed by the context. The Guild-house (p. 153) and housing for Brighton Beach were so lightly peppered with mannerist evocations as to be almost indistinguishable from their pattern sources. Under the circumstances, Philip Johnson's adjudication of the Venturi and Rauch submission for the Brighton Beach competition (1968) '. . . we [Johnson, Sert, Abrams and Ratensky] felt that the buildings looked like the most ordinary apartment construction built all over Queen's and Brooklyn since the Depression . . .'[84] is understandable. Other projects, notably the North Canton group (pp. 154–5) and the Frug House (scheme II, p. 157), are heavily spiced with Mannerist devices which readily distinguish them from their vernacular counterparts. A spiritual precedent to Robert Venturi's appreciation of the commonplace can be discovered in the London County Council's 'people's detailing' of the early fifties which resorted to the English *picturesque* as a means of differentiating architecture from the vernacular domestic landscape.

*Complexity and Contradiction in Architecture* is much more than a critique of orthodox modern architecture; it is to a large extent an historical justification of mannerism. Although Venturi seldom applies all the mannerist inflexions alluded to in the text to any single project (they are used with extreme circumspection and sensitivity), his point of view is pervasively Mannerist. Venturi's architecture is extraordinarily ordinary and its subject is pop. Both pop art and mannerist architecture impart an uncommon meaning to common elements of experience by manipulating psychic and architectural conventions. Venturi's originality arises from his discovery of the concurrence of pop art and mannerist architecture and their suitability as a means of enhancing meaning without undue risk of separating architecture from reality. The architect's enthusiasm for humble materials and sensible construction tends to

1. Fountain, Fairmont Park Art Association, Philadelphia. Competition entry, 1964.
As a terminal feature of the Benjamin Franklin Parkway, the fountain acquired an added dimension as traffic architecture.

mask the subtle sensitivity of his design contribution. The front façade of the Guild-house was purposely separated from the back at the top in order to emphasize its role as a street façade or public mask. The architects introduced free-standing walls and a false front in their North Canton Town Center (Ohio) to mediate between the civic and architectural scales by a thoughtful juxtaposition of contradictory fenestrations. These pseudo-functional walls perform a similar role to the real chair in Rauschenberg's painting *Pilgrim*.

Venturi noted that 'the surface pattern continues from the stretcher canvas to the actual chair in front of it, making ambiguous the distinction between painting and the furniture, and on another level, the work of art in a room'.[85] The false walls and fronts link the civic scale of the public street and plaza with the smaller semi-private scale pertaining to the architecture. Venturi repeated Louis Sullivan's use of the giant arch in the Guild-house and North Canton Town Hall as a device for registering civic scale and communal functions. In both buildings, he stressed the dichotomy of front and back which is a conspicuous feature of the main streets of mid-western United States towns.

The conception of architectural space as richly layered, with each layer obtaining a level of significance and functional relevance dictated by the contradictory demands of inside and outside, fascinates Robert Venturi and his associates. The external and

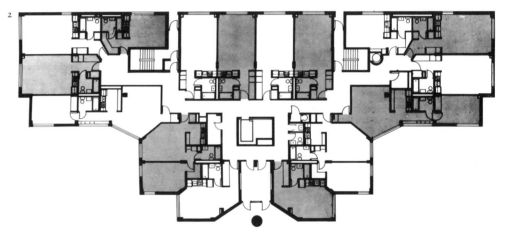

2, 3. Guild-house, Philadelphia, 1960–3.
2. Plan, Friends Housing for the Elderly.
3. Separated from the back at the roof parapet to further emphasize its vestigial role as a street façade.

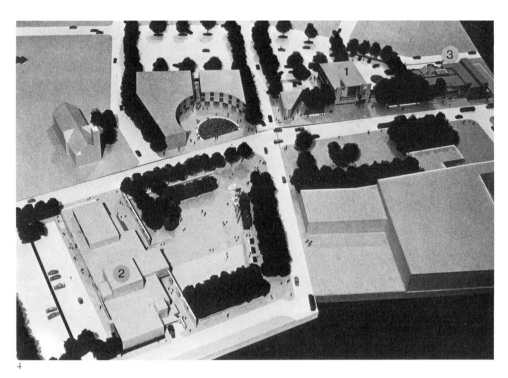

4

4. Three buildings for North Canton, Ohio.
Project, 1965–6. View of model. Key: 1 Town Hall,
2 YMCA Community Center, 3 Public Library.

5–8. Town Hall. Project, 1965.
5. Sketch.
6. Side view of model.
7. Frontal view of free-standing civic façade.
8. Plan, ground floor.

9–12. YMCA Community Center. Project, 1965.
9. North elevation.
10. View of model looking south.
11. Plan, lower floor.
12. Sketch view of corridor between free-standing plaza façade and building face.

13–15. Library addition. Project, 1965.
13. View of model looking east.
14. Section.
15. Plan, main floor.

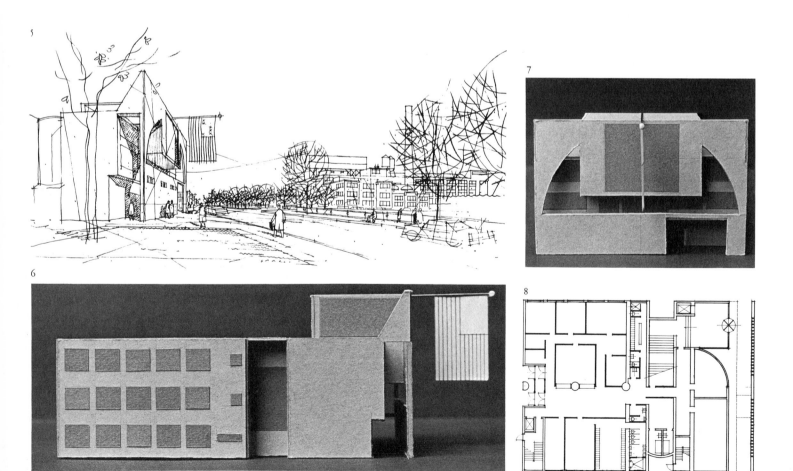

5

6

7

8

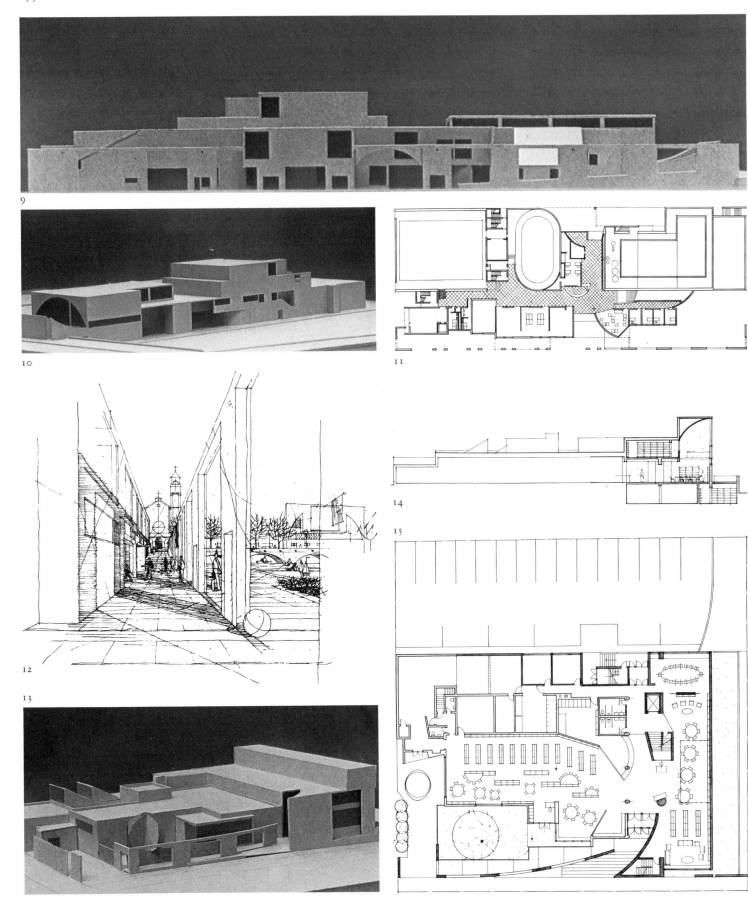

9

10

11

12

13

14

15

internal forms attributed to the Fountain competition entry for Philadelphia Fairmont Park Art Association (p. 153) demonstrated at an elementary level the accommodation of these contradictory demands. Jørn Utzon's design of the external weatherproof vaults and internal acoustic shells for the Sydney Opera House (1956–67, pp. 50–3) showed a similar regard for the different internal and external functions. Venturi and Rauch introduced a further sophistication into the Frug House schemes in which a pseudo-hood over the fireplace and juxtaposed walls (scheme II) created a feeling of multiple enclosure.

Quite often Venturi and Rauch develop hybrid concepts. The football Hall of Fame (p. 158) combined a bill-board and a building. In their competition scheme for the Franklin Delano Roosevelt Memorial (1960), they mated architecture to the landscape.

The television antennae atop the Guild-house, the giant flag draped in front of the North Canton Town Hall and the great bill-board towering over the football Hall of Fame attest to Venturi and Rauch's recognition of iconology as a prominent characteristic of the commercial landscape.

The adoption of pseudo-functional ornaments instanced by the television antennae highlights both the problem and the significance of pseudo elements in their architecture.

The dedication of Venturi and Rauch to the implementation of an architecture which is 'ugly and ordinary' and their identification with pop culture challenges the view of architecture as the prerogative of a cultured elite.

16, 17. Frug House, Princeton, N.J., Scheme I.
16. Section.
17. Back view of model.

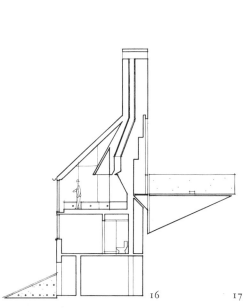

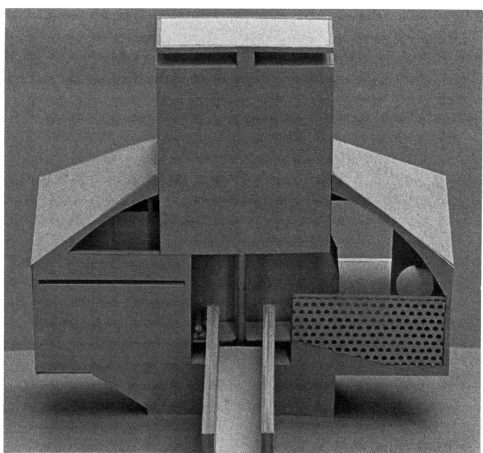

16          17

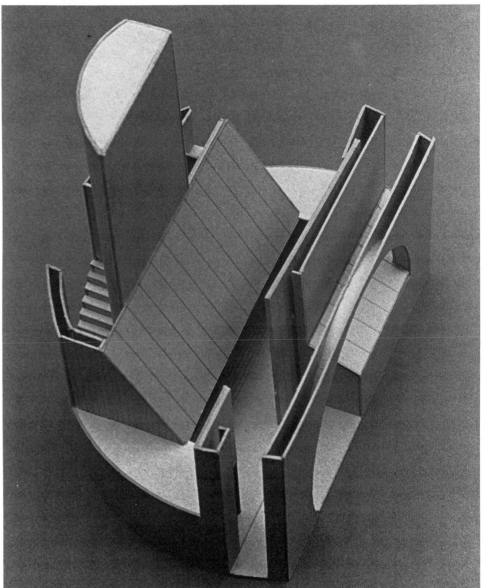

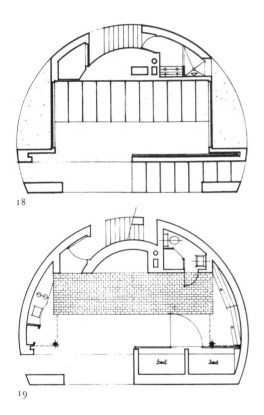

18

19

20

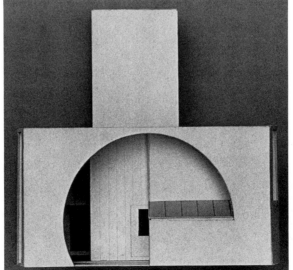

21

18–21. Frug House, Princeton, N.J., Scheme II.
18. Plan, upper level.
19. Plan, floor level.
20. View of model with flat roof removed to reveal double-front façade.
21. View of model, front façade.

22

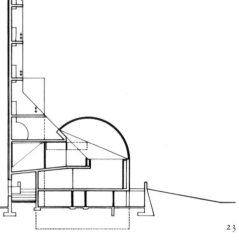

23

24

22–25. The National Football Foundation Hall of
Fame, New Brunswick, N.J. Project, 1966.
22. View of model, bill board façade.
23. Section.
24. Montage.
25. Rear view of model.

25

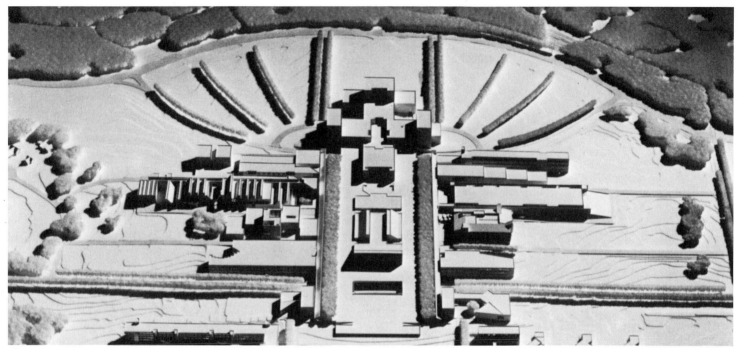

26

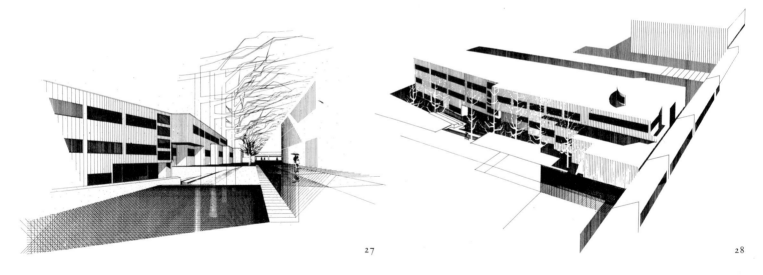

27

28

29

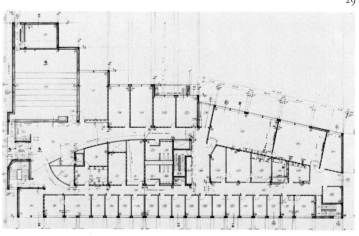

26–29. Social Sciences Building, State University
of New York. Project, 1970.
26. Aerial view of model.
27. Perspective view looking east towards the
university mall.
28. Aerial perspective.
29. Plan.

# Kevin Roche and John Dinkeloo

Kevin Roche was born in Dublin in 1922, and emigrated to the United States (1948) three years after graduating from the Ireland National University. Prior to joining Saarinen's office in 1950, he worked in London, Chicago and New York. Although only three years older than Robert Venturi, Kevin Roche's orthodoxy contrasts with Venturi's inclusive ideal of architecture. (Venturi also worked in Saarinen's office for a time (1954).) In 1961, Roche entered into partnership with John Dinkeloo to continue Saarinen's office after the latter's death. The practice is now made up of a staff of ninety, located at Hamden, Connecticut.

John Dinkeloo is a native American, born and trained in Michigan. He graduated from the University of Michigan in engineering and architecture (1942) and worked in the Chicago office of Skidmore, Owings and Merrill before joining Saarinen in 1950. Dinkeloo is a technical innovator who is credited with the development of structural neoprene gaskets for curtain walls, the use of laminated metalized glass for reducing heat loss in buildings, and the use of weathered exposed steel for the John Deere and Company headquarters building (Illinois).

On Eero Saarinen's death in 1961, Kevin Roche, his chief design assistant, and John Dinkeloo were entrusted with the stewardship of the practice. Saarinen was a master of architectural overstatement. He heightened the emotional impact of his forms by a deliberate resort to expressionism. It was his conviction 'that once one embarks on a concept for a building, *this concept has to be exaggerated and overstated and repeated in every part* so that . . . the building sings with the message'. (author's italics)[86] Overstatement and structural exhibitionism were techniques which Saarinen employed to express the essence of a building. Roche continues to design within the spirit of Saarinen's expressionism, although his imagery is alloyed with the cool abstract geometry of Mies. Though structural gymnastics and sensationalism are notably absent, Roche shares with Saarinen a predilection for overstatement.

However, the conscious understatement of the Oakland Museum (pp. 170–1), an early independent Kevin Roche design, seemed to point away from Saarinen's expressionism. It is the antithesis of Saarinen's architecture—a cool anonymous building which focuses on people and their activities rather than on a muscular imagery. The museum returns the land to its roofs through a series of terraced gardens and courtyards in a kind of anti-monumental 'non-building'. In succeeding designs, Roche has worked towards a closer rapport with Saarinen's aggressive expressionism, interpreted in a personal blend of John Deere and Mies.

The grotesque enlargement of the four brick corner pylons, improbable *épaulettes* to the Knights of Columbus tower (pp. 164–5), confers material strength to a slight torso. Backed by the legion bulk of the coliseum roof, this mute cyclops guards the principal motor approach to New Haven. Whereas the Oakland Museum is underplayed, the Knights of Columbus tower assumes an excessive scale unrelated to the city. The rectitude of Roche's statement incites a powerful emotional response akin to that evoked by Saarinen, which projects the nature of the building.

Mies provided a focus for Roche's stylistic evolution which served as a counterfoil to Saarinen's dynamic imagery. Somewhere between the attractions of these two expressionist polarities, Roche was able to define his sovereign interests.

The Cummins Engine Company offices and factory (pp. 162–3) represents the closest approach to Mies work in Roche's path to self-realization. The calculated woodiness and persistent trabeated motif of Roche's steel betrays Mies' ascetic discipline. From Cummins on, Roche maintained a delicate adjustment between a minimal geometry and an overtly sensuous full-bodied expression of structure.

*Buildings and Projects*

Richard C. Lee High School, New Haven, Connecticut, 1963–9
Oakland Museum, Oakland, California, 1964–9
Ford Foundation Headquarters Building, New York, 1965–8
Knights of Columbus Headquarters Building, New Haven, Connecticut, 1966–70
Cummins Engine Company, Darlington, England, 1964–7
Orangery
College Life Insurance Company of America, office complex, Indianapolis, Indiana, 1968–72
National Center for Higher Education, Washington, D.C.
Coliseum, New Haven, Connecticut, 1969–72

1, 2. Richard C. Lee High School, New Haven,
Connecticut, 1963–9.
1. View from south.
2. Plan, second floor.

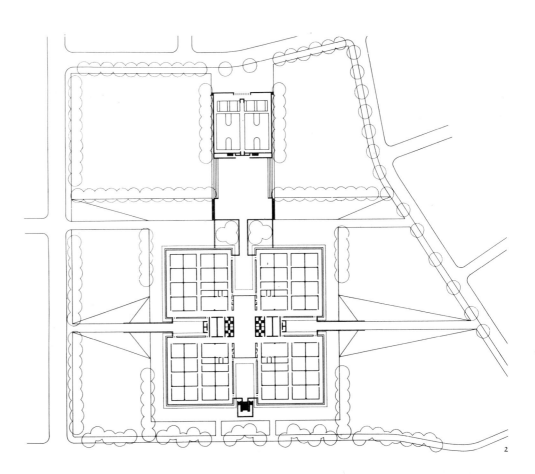

3–5. Cummins Engine Company, Darlington, England, 1964–7.
3. Plan, machine shop and administration areas.
4. A refined and expressive handling of Corten steel details strengthens the formal power of the architecture.
5. Sectional view reveals the hierarchy of steel-carpentry details.

3

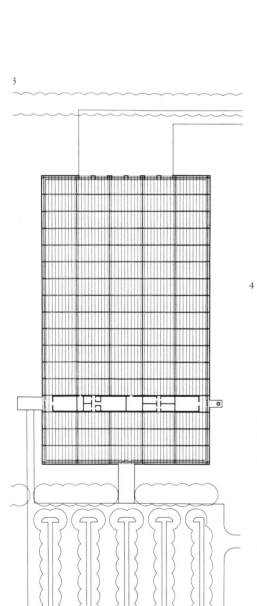

4

Three projects, the Ford Foundation Headquarters Building (pp. 166–7), the National Center for Higher Education (p. 168) and the College Life Insurance office complex (p. 169) explored the plastic potential of office towers wrapped around a vertical core space. Wright's Larkin Administration Building in Buffalo (1906) belongs to the same species of space. The stacked office floors opened onto a central core which penetrated the full height of the building. In the Ford Foundation, Roche shifted the vertical core onto the outside walls, to form an angled block of offices. The staggered office floors overlook a formally landscaped garden which serves as an entrance vestibule lit by a glazed roof. This theme was repeated in the College Life Insurance office towers. In the National Center for Higher Education, Roche deployed the offices around a triangular core space circular at the base and open at the apex.

A minor classical exercise, the design of an Orangery for a large estate (p. 171), complete with *grande allée*, summoned a forthright expression of Roche's Neo-classicism. The juxtaposition of exterior and interior forms, the contrast between the strongly-proportioned cube exterior and the hollowed-out layered interior with its apsoidal panel and skylight establishes a pulsating contrapuntal rhythm. Roche's exclusivist approach to architecture sets aside the complexity and contradiction implicit in life. He stands in direct contrast to Robert Venturi, and the popularist concerns of the third generation.

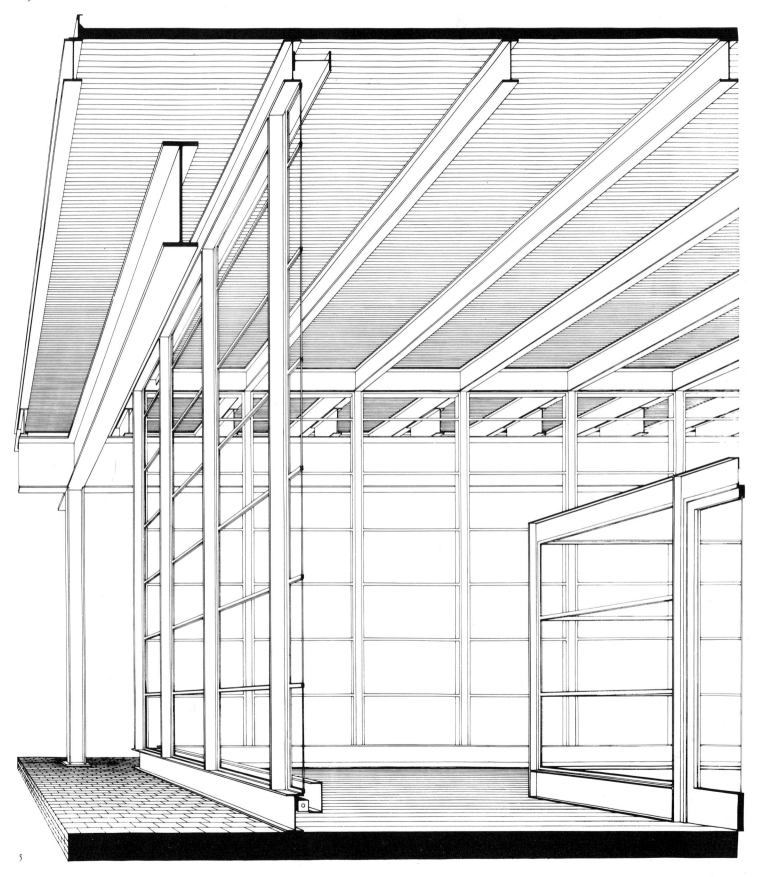

6

7

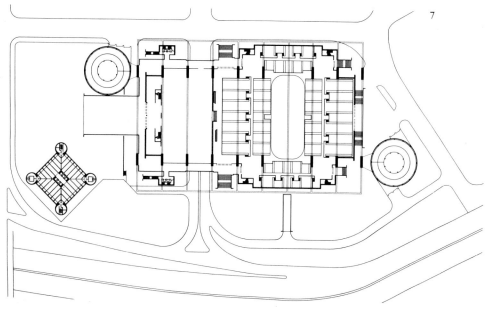

6–11. Knights of Columbus Headquarters Building, New Haven, Connecticut, 1966–70.
6. The building tower guards the main motor approach to New Haven.
7. Plan. Knights of Columbus tower (bottom left), new coliseum and parking ramps (centre).
8. Axonometric of the tower structure.
9. Vertical section of the Corten steel fenestration.
10. The image of American commercial power was amplified by the giant brick corner piers.
11. Interior, office suite.

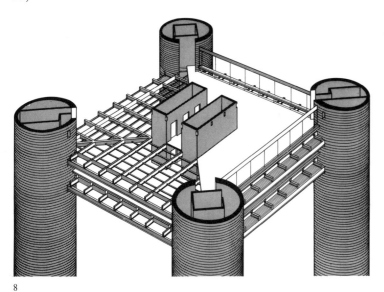

8

10

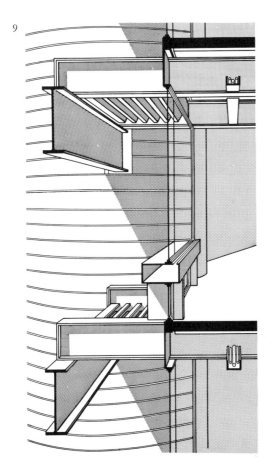

9

11

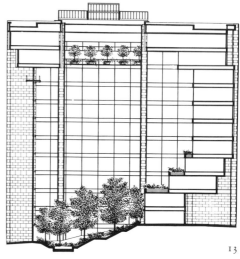

12–16. Ford Foundation Headquarters Building,
Manhattan Island, New York, 1965–8.
12. View from south-east.
13. Section through interior garden court.
14. Plan, street level.
15. Plan, tenth floor.
16. View, upper level of the garden court,
looking down into the north office wing.

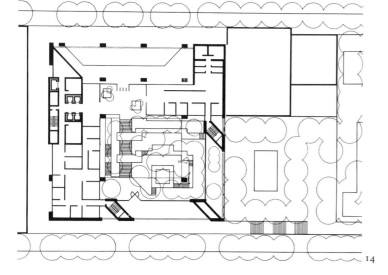

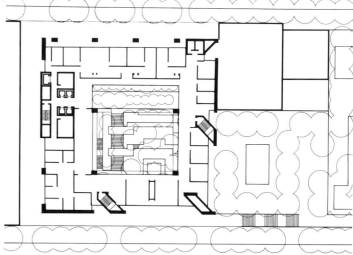

17

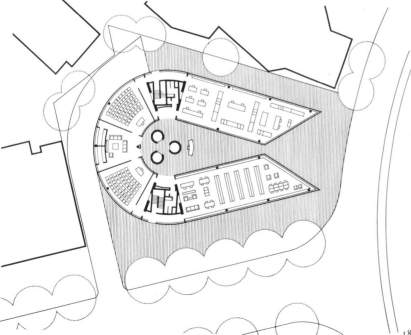

18

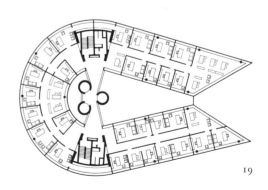

19

17–19. National Center for Higher Education, Washington, D.C. Project.
17. View of model.
18. Plan, ground floor.
19. Plan, typical floor.

20

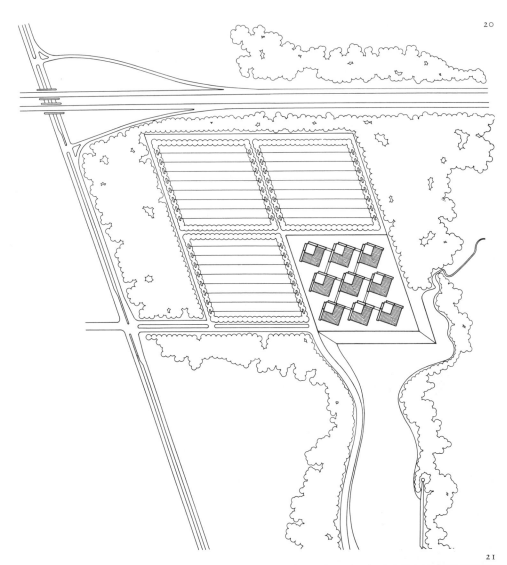

20, 21. College for Life Insurance Company of
America, Indianapolis, Indiana. Project, 1968–72.
20. Site development plan.
21. Rendering of the inclined mirror glass
façades.

21

22

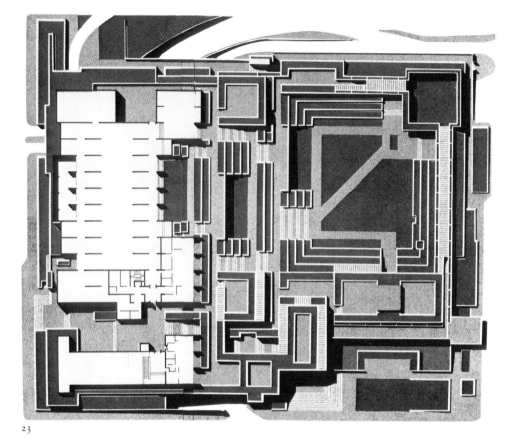

23

24

22–25. Oakland Museum, Oakland, California, 1964–9.
22. Section.
23. Plan of art museum and environs.
24. View of street access to the art museum.
25. View of museum terraces and garden courts.

25

26, 27. Orangery. Project.
26. Section.
27. Impressionistic rendering.

27

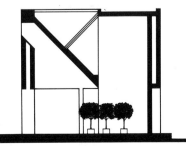

26

## Notes

[1] As quoted by Harrison Brown, *The Challenge of Man's Future*, New York 1954.

[2] Le Corbusier, *Towards a New Architecture*, London and New York 1970 (paperback), p. 210.

[3] *Op. cit.*, p. 210.

[4] Moshe Safdie, *Beyond Habitat*, Cambridge, Mass. 1970, p. 114.

[5] John Kenneth Galbraith, *The New Industrial State*, London and New York 1967, p. 396.

[6] Warren Chalk, 'Architecture as Consumer Product', *The Japan Architect* (Tokyo), 165 (1970, 7), p. 37.

[7] Paul Ehrlich, 'Playboy Interview', *Playboy* (Chicago), 1970, 8, p. 62.

[8] As quoted by J. M. Richards, 'Gourna: A Lesson in Basic Architecture', *The Architectural Review* (London), 876 (1970, 2), p. 110.

[9] Moshe Safdie, *op. cit.*, p. 74.

[10] Paul Ehrlich, *op. cit.*

[11] Hudson Hoagland, 'Cybernetics of Population Control', *Bulletin of the Atomic Scientists*, February 1964. Reprinted in *Population in Perspective*, edited by Louise B. Young, Oxford 1968, p. 392.

[12] Desmond Morris, *The Naked Ape*, London and New York 1967, p. 241.

[13] Lewis Mumford, *Technics and Civilization*, London and 8th Imp. 1962, p. 429.

[14] Quoted by Werner Heisenberg in *Physics and Beyond*, translated from the German by Arnold J. Pomeraus, London 1971.

[15] Ernst Cassirer, *Language and Myth*, New York 1946, p. 6.

[16] Christopher Alexander, 'The Environment', *The Japan Architect* (Tokyo), 165 (1970, 7), p. 52.

[17] *Op. cit.*, p. 52.

[18] Terence E. Lee, 'Human Needs and the Built Environment', *The Northern Architect*, July 1967, p. 826.

[19] Christian Norberg-Schulz, *Intentions in Architecture*, London and Cambridge, Mass. 1965, p. 76.

[20] *Op. cit.*, p. 42.

[21] Frederick Gutheim, Ed., *Frank Lloyd Wright on Architecture*, New York and London 1941, p. 63.

[22] Bernard Rudofsky, *Architecture Without Architects*, New York 1965, p. 3.

[23] Aldo van Eyck, 'A Miracle of Moderation', in Charles Jencks and George Baird, Eds., *Meaning in Architecture*, London and New York 1969, p. 183.

[24] Bernard Rudofsky, *op. cit.*

[25] Gunter Nitschke, 'Ma: The Japanese Sense of Place', *Architectural Design* (London), 1966, 3, p. 125.

[26] Christopher Alexander, *Notes on the Synthesis of Form*, Cambridge, Mass. 1964 (4th ed.), p. 30.

[27] Aldo van Eyck, *op. cit.*

[28] Françoise Choay, 'Urbanism and Semiology', in Charles Jencks and George Baird, Eds., *Meaning in Architecture*, London and New York 1969, p. 31.

[29] Aldo van Eyck, 'Team 10 Primer', *Architectural Design* (London), 1962, 12, p. 559.

[30] Reyner Banham, *Theory and Design in the First Machine Age*, London and New York 1960, p. 329.

[31] Christian Norberg-Schulz, *op. cit.*

[32] Reyner Banham, *op. cit.*

[33] Paul Rudolph, in *Perspecta 7, The Yale Architectural Journal* (New Haven, Conn.), 1962, p. 51.

[34] Aldo van Eyck, 'Team 10 Primer', *op. cit.*, p. 601.

[35] Peter and Alison Smithson, 'Team 10 Primer', *op. cit.*, p. 568.

[36] Forrest Wilson, 'From Product to Process: The Third Generation of Modern Architects', *Progressive Architecture* (Stamford, Conn.), 1970, 6, p. 157.

[37] Peter Carter, 'Mies van der Rohe', *Architectural Design* (London), 1961, 3, p. 115.

[38] Le Corbusier, *op. cit.*, p. 187.

[39] Reyner Banham, *op. cit.*, p. 272.

[40] Reyner Banham, *op. cit.*, p. 130.

[41] Le Corbusier and François de Pierrefeu, *The Home of Man*, London 1948, (F. 1942), p. 124.

[42] *Op. cit.*

[43] August Heckscher, *The Public Happiness*, New York 1962, p. 102.

[44] Robert Venturi, *Complexity and Contradiction in Architecture*, New York 1966, p. 46.

[45] Herman Hertzberger, 'Montessori Primary School in Delft, Holland', *Harvard Educational Review*, Vol. 39, No. 4, 1964, p. 66.

[46] Sigfried Giedion, *Space, Time and Architecture*, Cambridge, Mass. 1967, p. 668.

[47] Reyner Banham, 'On Trial 2: Louis Kahn', *The Architectural Review* (London), 781 (1962, 3), p. 205.

[48] Sigfried Giedion, *op. cit.*

[49] *Op. cit.*

[50] *Op. cit.*

[51] Bernard Rudofsky, *op. cit.*

[52] Le Corbusier, *The Four Routes*, London 1947, p. 136.

[53] Quoted by Reyner Banham, *The New Brutalism*, London and New York 1966, p. 46.

[54] *Op. cit.*, p. 62.

[55] Charles Jencks, 'Pop-Non Pop', *Architectural Association Quarterly*, Vol. 1, No. 2, April 1969, p. 57.

[56] *Op. cit.*, p. 52.

[57] Robert Venturi, *op. cit.*, p. 102.

[58] Marshall McLuhan, *Hot and Cold*, edited by Gerald Emanuel Stearn, Harmondsworth 1968, p. 62.

[59] Reyner Banham, *Theory and Design in the First Machine Age*, *op. cit.*, p. 329.

[60] Jørn Utzon, 'The Sydney Opera House', *Zodiac 14* (Milan), 1965, p. 49.

[61] Jørn Utzon, 'Platforms and Plateaux: Ideas of a Danish Architect', *Zodiac 10* (Milan), 1962, p. 116.

[62] *Op. cit.*, p. 116.

[63] Sigfried Giedion, *op. cit.*

[64] Robert Venturi, *op. cit.*, p. 71.

[65] Christopher Alexander, 'The Environment', *The Japan Architect* (Tokyo), 165 (1970, 7), p. 54.

[66] Moshe Safdie, *op. cit.*, p. 243.

[67] *Op. cit.*, p. 150.

[68] A. E. Komendant, 'Post-Mortem on Habitat', *Progressive Architecture* (Stamford, Conn.), 1968, 3, p. 147.

[69] Noboru Kawazoe, 'The City of the Future', *Zodiac 9* (Milan), 1962, pp. 99–112.

[70] John Donat, Ed., *World Architecture 2*, London 1965, p. 13.

[71] Arata Isozaki, 'Festival Plaza', *The Japan Architect* (Tokyo), 164 (1970, 5/6), p. 57.

[72] Peter Cook, 'Archigram 1970–71', *Architectural Design* (London), 1971, 8, p. 486.

[73] Warren Chalk, *op. cit.*, p. 37.

[74] Reyner Banham, *Theory and Design in the First Machine Age*, *op. cit.*, p. 330.

[75] Frei Otto, 'Clamps', *Architectural Design* (London), 1971, 3, p. 151.

[76] Paul Rudolph, *op. cit.*, p. 51.

[77] Bernard Lafaille, designer of the French Pavilion at Zagreb in Yugoslavia in 1935 (a single cartwheel of cables) and quoted approvingly by Frei Otto in 'Tents as Ideal Buildings', *The Japan Architect* (Tokyo), 165 (1970, 7), p. 38.

[78] Frei Otto and Peter Stromeyer, 'Pneumatic Structures', *American Institute of Architects Journal* (Washington, D.C.), 1962, 4, p. 111.

[79] James Stirling, 'Garches to Jaoul', *The Architectural Review* (London), 705 (1955, 9), p. 151.

[80] 'James Stirling in Tokyo, Interviewed by Arata Isozaki', *Architecture and Urbanism*, Vol. 1, No. 8, 1971, p. 7.

[81] *Op. cit.*, p. 6.

[82] James Stirling, 'Architects' Approach to Architecture', *Zodiac 16* (Milan), 1966, p. 161.

[83] *Op. cit.*, p. 167.

[84] Philip Johnson, letter to Jason R. Nathan, Administrator, Housing and Development Administration, City of New York, 12 March 1968. Quoted by Robert Stern in *New Directions in American Architecture*, London and New York, 1969, p. 10.

[85] Robert Venturi, *op. cit.*, p. 40; see also plate 43.

[86] Raymond Lifchez, 'On Eero Saarinen', *Zodiac 17* (Milan), 1967, p. 121.

## Bibliography

### Chapter 1

Georg Borgstrom, *Too Many, A Study of the Earth's Biological Limitations*, London 1969.

Rachel Carson, *Silent Spring*, London 1963.

Barry Commoner, *The Closing Circle*, London 1972.

'A Blueprint For Survival', *The Ecologist*, Vol. 2 (1972, 1), pp. 1–42.

Paul Ehrlich, *The Population Bomb*, London 1971.

Paul Ehrlich and Anne Ehrlich, *Population, Resources, Environment—Issues in Human Ecology*, San Francisco 1970.

Nan Fairbrother, *New Lives, New Landscapes*, London 1970.

Jay W. Forrester, *World Dynamics*, Cambridge, Mass. 1971.

Jay W. Forrester, 'Alternatives to Catastrophe, Understanding the Counterintuitive Behaviour of Social Systems', *The Ecologist*, Part 1: Vol. 1, No. 14, 1971; Part 2: Vol. 1, No. 15, 1971.

J. K. Galbraith, *The New Industrial State*, London and New York 1967.

Edward T. Hall, *The Hidden Dimension*, London 1966.

Thomas Malthus, *An Essay on the Principle of Population*, edited by Anthony Flew. Published in London 1970.

Ian L. McHarg, *Design with Nature*, New York 1969.

Lewis Mumford, *Technics and Civilization*, London 1934.

Lewis Mumford, *The City in History*, London 1961.

Lewis Mumford, *Pentagon of Power*, London 1971.

Louise B. Young, Ed., *Population in Perspective*, Oxford 1968.

### Chapter 2

Edward T. Hall, *The Hidden Dimension*, London 1966.

Charles Jencks and George Baird, Eds., *Meaning in Architecture*, London and New York 1969.

Marshall McLuhan, *The Gutenberg Galaxy*, London 1962.

Marshall McLuhan, *Hot and Cold*, edited by Gerald Emmanuel Stearn, Harmondsworth 1968.

Paul Oliver, Ed., *Shelter and Society*, London 1969.

Christian Norberg-Schulz, *Intentions in Architecture*, London and Cambridge, Mass. 1965.

### Selected Writings by Christopher Alexander

An acquaintance with the writings of Christopher Alexander is essential for an understanding of the theoretical interests of the third generation. He provides a cogent and integrated approach to the environment, coincidental with the mainstream of third-generation theory.

Christopher Alexander and Serge Chermayeff, *Community and Privacy—Toward a New Architecture of Humanism*, London and New York 1963.

C. Alexander, *Notes on the Synthesis of Form*, Cambridge, Mass. 1968.

C. Alexander, S. Ishikawa, M. Silverstein, *A Pattern Language which Generates Multi-Service Centers*, Center for Environmental Structure, Berkeley, Cal. 1968.

C. Alexander, S. Hirshen, S. Ishikawa, C. Coffin, S. Angel, *Houses Generated By Patterns*, Center for Environmental Structure, Berkeley, Cal. 1970.

C. Alexander, 'A City is not a Tree', *Architectural Forum* (New York), 1965, 4, pp. 58–62; and 1965, 5, pp. 58–61. A revised version of the article appeared in *Design* (London), 206 (1966, 2).

C. Alexander, 'The Theory and Invention of Form', *Architectural Record* (New York), 1965, April, pp. 177–84.

C. Alexander, 'The Pattern of Streets', *Architectural Design* (London), 1967, 11, pp. 528–31.

C. Alexander, 'Centre for Environmental Studies', *Architectural Design* (London), 1968, 5, pp. 204–5.

C. Alexander, 'Thick-Wall Pattern', *Architectural Design* (London), 1968, 7, pp. 324–6.

C. Alexander, 'Systems Generating Systems', *Architectural Design* (London), 1968, 12, pp. 605–10. This article first appeared in *Systemat*, the Journal of Inland Steel Products Company, Milwaukee.

C. Alexander, 'Major Changes in Environmental Form Required by Social and Psychological Demands', *Ekistics*, Vol. 28, No. 165 (August 1969), pp. 78–85.

C. Alexander, 'Change of Form', *Architectural Design* (London), 1970, 3, pp. 122–5. This article was based on a paper presented at the Second International Symposium on Regional Development, Japan Centre for Area Development Research, September 17–19 1968, Tokyo.

C. Alexander, 'Center for Environmental Structure', [submission in the International Competition for Low-Cost Housing, Lima, Peru], *Architectural Design* (London), 1970, 4, pp. 193–6.

C. Alexander, 'The Environment', *The Japan Architect* (Tokyo), 165 (1970, 7), pp. 52–4.

Geoffrey Broadbent, 'A Plain Man's Guide to Systematic Design Methods', *RIBA Journal*, May 1968, pp. 223–7.

Roger Montgomery, 'Pattern Language', *Architectural Forum* (New York), 1970, 1, pp. 52–9.

Chapter 3

'A View of Contemporary World Architecture', Special edition, *The Japan Architect* (Tokyo), July 1970.

Reyner Banham, *Theory and Design in the First Machine Age*, London and New York 1960.

Reyner Banham, *The New Brutalism*, London and New York 1966.

Sigfried Giedion, *Space, Time and Architecture*, Cambridge, Mass. 1967.

John Jacobus, *Twentieth Century Architecture: The Middle Years 1940–65*, London and New York 1966.

Charles Jencks, *Architecture 2000*, London 1971.

Charles Jencks, 'Pop-Non Pop', *Architectural Association Quarterly*, Vol. 1, No. 1, winter 1968/69, pp. 48–63; Vol. 1, No. 2, April 1969, pp. 56–74.

Jürgen Joedicke, *Architecture since 1945*, London and Stuttgart 1969.

Lewis Mumford, 'The Case against Modern Architecture', *Architectural Record* (New York), Vol. 131, No. 4, 1962, pp. 155–9.

Bernard Rudofsky, *Architecture Without Architects*, New York 1965.

Peter and Alison Smithson, 'Team 10 Primer', *Architectural Design* (London), Dec. 1962.

Robert Venturi, *Complexity and Contradiction in Architecture*, New York 1966.

Forrest Wilson, 'From Product to Process: The Third Generation of Modern Architects', *Progressive Architecture* (Stamford, Conn.), 1970, 6, pp. 156–67.


Selected Writings by and about the Architects

John Andrews

J. Andrews, 'Beyond Individual Building', *Architectural Record* (New York), September 1966, pp. 161–72.

J. Andrews, 'The Focus is People', *The Japan Architect* (Tokyo), 165 (1970, 7), pp. 44–5.


Archigram

*Archigram I*, 'Flow and Expendability' (Greene, Cook, Webb), 1961.

*Archigram II*, 'Expendability and Change' (Greene, Cook, Webb + Herron, Chalk, Crompton), 1962.

*Archigram III*, 'Expendability', 1963.

*Archigram IV*, 'Plug-in', 1964.

*Archigram V*, 'An International Survey of Sympathetic Ideas', 1965.

*Archigram VI*, 'Prefabrication in England in the Nineteen-forties', 1966.

*Archigram VII*, 'Control and Choice', 1967.

*Archigram VIII*, 'Beyond Architecture', 1967.

*Archigram IX*, 'Archizones, a grab bag of international contributions', 1970.

*Living City Exhibition Catalogue*, London, Institute of Contemporary Arts, June/August 1963.

Plug-in City article, *Sunday Times colour supplement*, London 1964.

Peter Cook, *Architecture: Action and Plan*, London and New York 1967.

Peter Cook, *Experimental Architecture*, London and New York 1970.


Kiyonori Kikutake

K. Kikutake and Noriaki Kurokawa, *Metabolism, Proposals for a New Urbanism*, Tokyo 1960.*

K. Kikutake, *Taisha Kenchikuran* [Metabolic Architecture], Tokyo 1968.*

K. Kikutake, *Ningen-no-Kenchiku* [Human Architecture], Tokyo 1970.*

K. Kikutake, *Ningen-no-Toshi* [A Human City], Tokyo 1970.*

K. Kikutake, 'Sky House', *World Architecture One*, Ed. John Donat, London 1964, pp. 20–25.

K. Kikutake, 'The Great Shrine of Izumo, Izumi-taisha-Chonoya', *World Architecture Two*, Ed. John Donat, London 1965, pp. 10–19.

* The book titles listed are Japanese editions.


Kisho Noriaki Kurokawa

K. N. Kurokawa and Kiyonori Kikutake, *Metabolism, Proposals for a New Urbanism*, Tokyo 1960.*

K. N. Kurokawa, *Prefabricated Concrete Component Housing*, Tokyo.*

K. N. Kurokawa, *Urban Design* (Kinokuniya Book), Tokyo.*

K. N. Kurokawa, *Action Architecture in Japan*, Tokyo.*

K. N. Kurokawa, 'The Architecture of Action', *Kenchiku Bunka* (Tokyo), 215 (1964, 9), pp. 69–100; and *Architectural Design* (London), 1964, 12, pp. 603–7.

K. N. Kurokawa, 'Metabolism: The Pursuit of Open Form', *World Architecture One*, Ed. John Donat, London 1964, pp. 10–13.

K. N. Kurokawa, 'Two Systems of Metabolism', *The Japan Architect* (Tokyo), 137 (1967, 12), pp. 80–82.

* The book titles listed are Japanese editions.


Frei Otto

Frei Otto, *Das hängende Dach: Gestalt und Struktur*, [Doctoral thesis], Berlin 1954.

Frei Otto, *Tensile Structures*, Vol. I, Cambridge, Mass. and London 1967.

Frei Otto, *Tensile Structures*, Vol. II, Cambridge, Mass. and London 1969.

Frei Otto and Peter Stromeyer, 'Tents', *American Institute of Architects Journal* (Washington, D.C.), 1961, 2, pp. 77–86.

Frei Otto and Peter Stromeyer, 'Pneumatic Structures', *American Institute of Architects Journal* (Washington, D.C.), 1962, 4, pp. 101–11. Originally published in *Deutsche Bauzeitung* (Stuttgart), 1962, 7, pp. 518–27.

Frei Otto, 'Imagination et Architecture—Essai d'une Vision de l'Avenir', *L'Architecture d'Aujourd'hui* (Boulogne), 102 (1962, 6/7), pp. 89–93.

Frei Otto, 'Tents as Ideal Buildings', *The Japan Architect* (Tokyo), 165 (1970, 7), pp. 38–9. Originally published in *Deutsche Bauzeitung* (Stuttgart), 1968.

Conrad Roland, *Frei Otto: Structures*, London and New York 1970.

Ludwig Glaeser, *The Work of Frei Otto*, New York 1972.


Moshe Safdie

M. Safdie, *Beyond Habitat*, Cambridge, Mass. 1970.

M. Safdie, 'A Case for City Living', [student thesis], *Forum* (Netherlands), February/March 1962, pp. 171–83.

M. Safdie, 'Industrial Buildings', *Canadian Architect*, October 1967, p. 17.

M. Safdie, 'New Environmental Requirements for Urban Building', *Zodiac 19* (Milan), 1969, pp. 181–2.

M. Safdie, 'The City that Could be', *The Japan Architect* (Tokyo), 165 (1970, 7), pp. 42–3.

A. E. Komendant, 'Post-Mortem on Habitat', *Progressive Architecture* (Stamford, Conn.), 1968, 3, pp. 138–47.


James Stirling

J. Stirling, 'Garches to Jaoul', *The Architectural Review* (London), 705 (1955, 9), pp. 145–51.

J. Stirling, 'Ronchamp—Le Corbusier's Chapel and the Crisis of Rationalism', *The Architectural Review* (London), 711 (1956, 3), pp. 155–61.

J. Stirling, 'A Personal View of the Present Situation', *Design* (London), March 1959.

J. Stirling, 'The Functional Tradition and Expression', *Perspecta 6*, *The Yale Architectural Journal* (New Haven, Conn.), 1960.

J. Stirling, 'Architects' Approach to Architecture', *Zodiac 16* (Milan), 1966, pp. 160–9.

J. Stirling, 'Anti-Structure', *Zodiac 18* (Milan), 1968, pp. 51–60.

J. Stirling, 'A Conversation with some American Students', *The Japan Architect* (Tokyo), 165 (1970, 7), pp. 32–33.

'James Stirling in Tokyo, Interviewed by Arata Isozaki', *Architecture and Urbanism*, Vol. 1, No. 8, 1971, pp. 4–16.

## Jørn Utzon

J. Utzon, 'Platforms and Plateaux: Ideas of a Danish Architect', *Zodiac 10* (Milan), 1962, pp. 112–41.

J. Utzon, 'The Sydney Opera House', *Zodiac 14* (Milan), 1965, pp. 48–93.

J. Utzon, 'Additive Architecture', *Arkitektur* (Copenhagen), 1970, 1, p. 1.

Elias Duek Cohen, Ed., *Utzon and the Sydney Opera House*, Sydney 1967.

## Robert Venturi

R. Venturi, *Complexity and Contradiction in Architecture*, New York 1966.

A summary of *Complexity and Contradiction in Architecture* was also published in *Zodiac 17* (Milan), 1967, pp. 122–6.

# Index

Page numbers in *italics* refer to illustrations

Aalto, Alvar 35, 37, 39, 40, 44; *36*
Abrams 152
Alexander, Christopher 7, 11, 18, 20, 21, 22, 24, 25, 28, 30, 31, 35, 43, 45, 48, 58, 59, 69, 78, 92, 102; *29, 30*
Allison, Ken *110, 111*
Andrews, John 12, 16, 38, 144ff; *18, 145ff*
Archigram Group 7, 12, 16, 18, 31, 42, 46, 48, 69, 80, 92, 102ff, 114, 115; *14, 103ff*
Arup Associates 45, 47, 69; *124*
Asplund, Gunnar 44
Atelier 5 40

Banham, Reyner 16, 27, 28, 31, 33, 37, 42, 43, 46, 102, 114, 130; *43*
Bauhaus 34, 38, 42; *39*
Behnisch & Partners *122, 123*
Bell, Alexander Graham *71*
Blake, Peter 42; *42*
Bohr, Niels 20
Bruegel, Piet 92
Burton, Decimus 130; *131*

Calhoun, John 18
Center for Environmental Structure 28, 30; *29*
Chalk, Warren 12, 102, 103; *108, 109*
Chareau, Pierre 131
Christian, John 17
Choay, Françoise 26
Clark, Gerod 152
Cook, Peter 58, 102; *105, 107, 110, 111*
Craig 22
Crompton, Dennis 102
Crosby, Theo 102

Dinkeloo, John 160ff; *161ff*
Doesburg, Theo van *28*

Eesteren, Cor van *28*
Ehrlich, Paul 14
English Independent Group 42
Eyck, Aldo van 24, 25, 31, 33, 40, 58

Faller & Schröder *19*
Fathy, Hassan 15; *17*
Forrester, Jay 19, 20
Fournier, Colin *110, 111*
Friedman, Yona 92
Fuller, Buckminster 15

Galbraith, John Kenneth 12
Geddes, Patrick 68
General Dynamics Corporation 115
Giedion, Sigfried 36–9*passim*, 44, 47, 134
Ginkel, Sandy van 58
Gowan, James 130, 131; *132–7*
Greene, David 102; *106, 110, 111*
Gropius, Walter 7, 10, 31, 33, 34, 38; *39*
Gutbrod, Rolf 114

Habraken, Nicholas 18, 19, 68, 78, 79
Heckscher, August 35
Henderson, Nigel 42
Herron, Ron 102; *106, 109–13*
Hertzberger, Hermann 36
Hudson, Hoagland 17
Humboldt, Wilhelm von 20

Institute for Lightweight Structure 114, 115
Institute of Contemporary Arts 102
Isozaki, Arata 90ff, 105, 130; *91ff*

Jencks, Charles 22, 42
Johnson, Philip 152
Joyce, James 41

Kahn, Louis 37, 58, 59, 68, 152; *16, 38*
Kaufmann, Edgar J. 28
Kawazoe, Noboru 68
Kikutake, Kiyonori 12, 18, 37, 58, 78ff, 90, 115; *40, 79ff*
Koestler, Arthur 22
Komendant, A. E. 59
Kurokawa, Kisho Noriaki 18, 58, 68ff, 92, 145; *69ff*

Laurens, Henri 44
Layer, Reinhold *19*
Le Corbusier 7, 10, 12, 28, 33–5*passim*, 37, 40, 44, 58, 68, 130, 131, 145, 150; *7, 11, 35, 37, 59*
Lee, Terence E. 21
Lee Whorf, Benjamin 21
Lennon, John 130
Lewis, Wyndham 41
Littlewood, Joan 90
Lyons, Israel & Ellis 130, 131

McHale, John 42
McLuhan, Marshall 41, 42
Martin, Sir Leslie 130, 134
Merrill—see Skidmore, Owings & Merrill
Metabolists 7, 13, 16, 31, 37, 38, 39, 40, 42, 68, 69, 70, 78, 79; *14, 40*
Meyer, Hannes 31, 34, 59
Mies van der Rohe 7, 15, 28, 33–5*passim*, 114, 116, 160; *34*
Mondrian, Piet 28
Morris, Desmond 18
Mumford, Lewis 19
Murano & Muri 78

Newby, Frank *110, 111*
Newton, Sir Isaac 117
Norberg-Schulz, Christian 22, 27

Otto, Frei 13, 15, 39, 42, 80, 114ff; *40, 115ff*
Owings—see Skidmore, Owings & Merrill

Paolozzi, Eduardo 42
Parent, Claude *13*
Parkin, J. B. 144
Piccard, Jacques 16
Pietilä, Reima 37; *39*

**Photo Credits**